Dugan / Villanova '86

D1091407

$0295H

Love for Love

THE NEW MERMAIDS

General Editors
PHILIP BROCKBANK
Professor of English, York University

BRIAN MORRIS
Senior Lecturer in English, York University

G. Kneller Bar.t pinx.t   T. Chambars sculp.

Love for Love

WILLIAM CONGREVE

Edited by M. M. KELSALL

ERNEST BENN LIMITED
LONDON

First published in this form 1969
by Ernest Benn Limited
Bouverie House · Fleet Street · London · EC4
© Ernest Benn Limited 1969
Distributed in Canada by
The General Publishing Company Limited · Toronto
Printed in Great Britain

510–33661–2

Paperback 510–33662–0

CONTENTS

ACKNOWLEDGEMENTS

IN EDITING the text I have made much use of Montague Summers' edition of *The Complete Works of William Congreve* (London, 1923), whose annotations are the fullest available, and the edition, by my much respected teacher and friend, the late Herbert Davis, of Congreve's *Complete Plays* (Chicago, 1967). Davis' text is based on extensive collation in England and the United States of the authoritative editions published in Congreve's lifetime. The textual apparatus printed here substantially corresponds with his, but further collation has enabled me to add to the list of variants. I am also indebted to Mr. Cedric Brown of the University College of Swansea for help in tracing some of the more obscure astrologers and astronomers.

INTRODUCTION

THE AUTHOR

WILLIAM CONGREVE was born at Bardsey in Yorkshire on 24 January 1670.[1] He was educated in Ireland where his father went first as lieutenant in a company of foot, and later became resident agent for the Earl of Cork and Burlington. At Kilkenny College school he was a younger contemporary of Jonathan Swift, and from thence went, like Swift, to Trinity College, Dublin. He was enrolled 17 March 1691 as a law student in the Middle Temple, London.

Congreve had little intention of studying law. At Will's coffee house, Covent Garden, he became the associate of many of the leading literary figures of the day, in particular John Dryden, to whose translation of Juvenal and Persius (1693) he contributed a version of Juvenal's eleventh satire. His first comedy, *The Old Bachelor*, was produced at Drury Lane in March 1693. Dryden, who had helped in its preparation for the stage, called it the best first play he had seen; Thomas Southerne, the dramatist, recommended it to Thomas Davenant, the manager of the Theatre Royal; it ran for the unusual length for those times of fourteen days. This was followed by *The Double Dealer* in November of the same year, *Love for Love* (1695), *The Mourning Bride*, a tragedy (1697), *The Way of the World* (1700), and a masque, *The Judgment of Paris* (1701). This was Congreve's last work as a playwright. Although his plays were soon established in the standard repertory, it has been said that Congreve gave up the theatre because he was disappointed in his public. Despite the immediate success of *The Old Bachelor* and *Love for Love*, his other comedies were at first caviare to the general. *The Double Dealer* only just escaped being hissed from the stage, his finest achievement, *The Way of the World*, was said not to 'answer expectation'; to be too keen in its satire to win general applause. But it has also been claimed that there was nothing further for him to achieve in comedy. He knew when his vein was exhausted; he had perfected his art in *The Way of the World* and his love of ease was greater than his ambition. 'Ease and quiet is what I hunt after,' he wrote. 'If I have not ambition, I have other passions more easily gratified.'

He lived thereafter as Voltaire described him 'upon no other foot

[1] The biographical information in this section is from J. C. Hodges, *William Congreve the Man: a Biography from New Sources* (New York, 1941).

than that of a gentleman, who led a life of plainness and simplicity.'[2]
He was not rich. His government sinecures did not pay well until,
after the accession of George I, his Whig friends obtained him a
commission as Secretary to the Island of Jamaica; his speculation
with Vanbrugh as joint manager of the new Haymarket theatre
(1704–05) was a failure; his share in Betterton's company in
Lincoln's Inn Fields proved of little value. He was, however, the
friend of the wits and of the great. He was one of the group which
met initially (at the expense of Tonson, the publisher) to consume
the mutton pies of Christopher Cat in Sheer Lane, from whence the
Kit-Cat club grew. He was the intimate, therefore, of Addison and
Steele, Burlington, Kneller, and Vanbrugh; he was a friend of Swift
and Pope, who dedicated his translation of the *Iliad* to him, and of
Lady Mary Wortley Montagu; he was the lover of Henrietta,
Duchess of Marlborough, with whom much of his time in his
declining years was spent. He died 19 January 1729 and was buried
in Westminster Abbey.

THE PLAY

Love for Love was finished before the end of 1694, but not performed until 30 April 1695, when it ran for thirteen days.[3] The
delay in production was largely occasioned by a quarrel within the
'United Company' at the Theatre Royal between the actors and
the patentees. Thomas Betterton, the foremost actor of the company,
broke with the patentees, and having secured a licence, established a
new playhouse in Lincoln's Inn Fields, carrying with him a sub-
stantial number of the principal players from the Theatre Royal.
Love for Love was chosen to open the new house. According to
Colley Cibber it 'ran on with such extraordinary success that they
had seldom occasion to act any other play till the end of the season.'[4]

Betterton acted Valentine, Anne Bracegirdle, the famous beauty
(and Congreve's mistress), was well suited to Angelica; the great
Elizabeth Barry, for whom Otway had created his most famous roles,
now no longer in the flower of youth, was cast as Mrs. Frail; Samuel
Sandford, a man 'diminutive, and mean, (being round-shouldered,
meagre-faced, spindle-shanked, splay-footed, with a sour countenance, and long lean arms)' was chosen as Foresight. The greatest

---

[2] *Letters Concerning the English Nation*, XIX.
[3] I am indebted for information on the stage history to E. L. Avery,
Congreve's Plays on the Eighteenth-Century Stage (New York, 1951).
[4] *An Apology for the Life of Colley Cibber*, ed. R. W. Lowe (London, 1889),
i, 197.

success, however, was achieved by Thomas Dogget as Ben, who, it was said, had taken lodgings in Wapping to get up his sailor's part. All the roles, however, were in the hands of experienced and talented players.

Love for Love was the most successful of Congreve's plays in the eighteenth century, and underwent the slowest eclipse in the nineteenth. Although performed every season from 1703–04 until 1766–67, it suffered, like the rest of Congreve's work, from the comparative neglect of David Garrick. There were no Congrevian roles in Garrick's finale of 1776, and although *Love for Love* bloomed awhile thereafter pruned by the chaste hand of Thomas Sheridan, it suffered the common fate of Restoration drama and withered in Victoria's England. The moral blasts of Jeremy Collier still blow in the Podsnappery of Thomas Babington Macaulay.

It seems Congreve's lot to have been always the centre of a moral controversy. The shade of Podsnap may now be at rest, but the severe winds of a new astringent moral scrutiny have blown up from East Anglia. In what is probably the best essay of academic criticism written on Restoration drama,[5] Congreve has been weighed in the balance against the mature comedy of Henry James and found wanting. Moreover, compared with twentieth-century writers (like Lawrence?) who have explored the relations between the sexes in new depth, Congreve's moral vision has been found superficial and cliché-ridden. He is, like the age, gross, trivial, and dull. Lamb's defence of the comedy of the Restoration, that because it is a world of high fantasy, it is outside moral consideration, has had little support.[6] Those who now admire Congreve have claimed that his work is a mirror of the times,[7] and when this has provoked the obvious rejoinder that his was merely a fragmented and superficial culture, the rumble has been heard of the heavy guns of Hobbes and Locke. The comedies have been seen as pursuing that union of judgment and fancy which is true wit,[8] or of seeking (even epistemologically) for some basis of value in personal relations in a deceptive and corrupt society. The case has been pushed to extremes; the plays

> end like a phallic orgy in some Mycenean village square, with a marriage; and these marriages, like the primal marriage of the heaven-father to the earth-mother, symbolize the closing of a gap,

[5] L. C. Knights, 'Restoration Comedy: The Reality and the Myth', in *Explorations: Essays in Criticism Mainly on the Literature of the Seventeenth Century* (1946), originally in *Scrutiny* VI (1937), 122–43.

[6] 'On the Artificial Comedy of the Last Age' in *The Essays of Elia* (1821).

[7] B. Dobrée, *Restoration Comedy* (Oxford, 1924).

[8] T. H. Fujimura, *The Restoration Comedy of Wit* (Princeton, 1952).

albeit the more abstract gap between appearance and nature, and between rational fact and irrational value.[9]

It is thus, one assumes, that the brightest star in the blue firmament shoots from above in a jelly of love (V, 336–8). Lest this should appear too pagan or too orgiastic a reading, it has been counterbalanced by the argument that *Love for Love* is a (secular) Christian allegory.[10] The heroine (after all) is called Angelica.

Amongst such diversity of opinion there is one common element. Like Jeremy Collier or Macaulay, the majority of those who have written on Congreve are serious and earnest.[11] Hence the neglect of Charles Lamb. Yet it was Lamb's advantage that he saw the plays of Congreve regularly acted in a theatrical tradition directly descended from Congreve's day. Whatever refinements of interpretation one may place on it, *Love for Love* is primarily a stage comedy and it is upon the theatrical effectiveness of action and style that it must mainly be judged. One instance may initially suffice:

MISS PRUE

> Look you here, madam, then, what Mr. Tattle has given me. Look you here, cousin, here's a snuff-box; nay, there's snuff in't;—here, will you have any?—O good! How sweet it is.—Mr. Tattle is all over sweet, his peruke is sweet, and his gloves are sweet, and his handkerchief is sweet, pure sweet, sweeter than roses.—Smell him, mother, madam, I mean. He gave me this ring for a kiss.   (II, 456–62)

This has little to do with Hobbes, Locke, Mycenean villages, Christian allegory, or moral uplift. But it is good theatre. The whole circle of actors upon the stage are drawn into the comedy: Miss Prue in triumphant rustic naivety now launched into the way of the world, about to take snuff (the most unladylike of habits), and remembering, almost, to call her stepmother madam; the ladies themselves recoiling from the odious snuff-box; sweet Mr. Tattle overwhelmed (perhaps) with embarrassment at Miss Prue's profession of his arts and proclamation of his seductive charms. Moreover, even Henry James does not always achieve a limpidity of expression to match this passage from Congreve; and, whatever the sexual insights to be gained in the woods near Wragby, D. H. Lawrence cannot always express the grossness of sensuality in prose at the same time so

[9] N. N. Holland, *The First Modern Comedies* (Cambridge, Mass., 1959).
[10] C. R. Lyons, 'Congreve's Miracle of Love', *Criticism* VI (1964), 331–48.
[11] But cp. the humane essays by Virginia Woolf in *The Moment* (1947), and the characteristic corruscations from John Wain in 'Restoration Comedy and its Modern Critics', *Essays in Criticism* VI (1956), 367–85.

physically suggestive and comically ridiculous. Miss Prue is indeed gross and trivial, but, surely, as a stage creation, she is not dull.

Although the judgment of stage drama in relation to the novel is of limited viability, the comparison with James, at least, is valuable. James found Congreve 'insufferable', but perhaps envy resides in proximity, for both were writers whose foremost concern was with the perfecting of their art. Praise has always been lavished by Congreve's admirers on the harmonies of his prose, but this concern for the lustre of language was merely one aspect of his Augustanism —his determination as a self-conscious dramatic craftsman to polish to its highest lustre matter traditionally given; not to make things new, but to make them with greater elegance. Hence, since his material is in its origin literary, from Terence, from Jonson or Molière, from the whole European tradition of classical comedy, he is a writer not concerned with holding the mirror up to his own society, which provides merely the local colouring for traditional stage action, but rather with holding the mirror up to Nature: that idealised world of neo-classical literary aspiration which art strove to create, although the Augustan usually claimed merely to imitate. The aim of the dramatist was to realise, in the artifact, perfect form, to create a world of ideal or universal types—what Lamb calls, in the sloppy language of Romantic criticism, first Utopia, and then a 'dream' world. When Congreve was not up on a high horse trying to defend himself from Collier by claiming a moral justification for his satire[12] —his defence everyone agrees is feeble—he writes as an artist, not as a moralist. He envies Terence because his material was given him (from Aristotle via Menander); and thus Terence, in his drama, could concentrate upon 'purity' of style, and 'justness' (conformity to type) of manners.[13] Congreve speaks in his own work of the problem of displaying and arranging each character, 'how much of it, what part of it to show in light, and what to cast in shades; how to set it off by preparatory scenes, and by opposing other humours to it in the same scene.'[14] He makes characters in order to display various extravagant 'humours' (dominant traits), or 'affectations' in manners or eccentricities in speech, but he does not explore the moral consciousness. He represents Nature; he is not a social historian. He does not see his plays as intellectual or epistemological dilemmas, but as artifacts in a traditional 'kind', the genre 'Comedy' as practised by his great predecessors.

Love for Love is probably the closest to 'pure' art of all his comedies. The triangle, lover, mistress, hostile father, was old even

---

[12] *Amendments of Mr. Collier's False and Imperfect Citations* (1698).
[13] Dedication of *The Way of the World*.
[14] *Concerning Humour in Comedy* (1696).

to Thespis. Terence would have called Jeremy, Davus. Miss Prue, the not so innocent country maid; Mrs. Frail, the ageing woman eager for marriage, are Restoration stock in trade. Even sailor Ben has his forefathers.[15] The astrologer, Foresight, the most famous of Congreve's humour characters, is a fabrication from literary theory. Social history may tell one something about the status of astrology in Congreve's day (even Dryden, a member of the Royal Society, cast horoscopes);[16] in the debunking of Foresight one may see something of the effect of the Enlightenment upon literature; and in the satire on false science one may find a rational purpose in the comedy—but Foresight is an imaginative fabrication, a creation of literary fantasy working from literary theory, a type, not a character one *recognises*, or if one recognises, only in the most general manner. The art is in the making of a stage personality which is projected; in providing a vehicle for the actor. There is no illusion that this is a real person whose inmost mind we come to know, perhaps better than he knows himself. It is extrovert and extravagant art, not introverted and morally exploratory:

FORESIGHT (*Looking in the glass*)

I do not see any revolution here. Methinks I look with a serene and benign aspect—pale, a little pale—but the roses of these cheeks have been gathered many years. Ha! I do not like that sudden flushing—gone already! Hem, hem, hem! faintish. My heart is pretty good—yet it beats; and my pulses, ha!—I have none— mercy on me! Hum—yes, here they are. Gallop, gallop, gallop, gallop, gallop, gallop, hey! Whither will they hurry me? Now they're gone again. And now I'm faint again; and pale again, and hem! and my hem!—breath, hem!—grows short; hem! hem! he, he, hem!

SCANDAL

It takes; pursue it in the name of love and pleasure.

(III, 528–38)

If this were 'real' it would not be comic. Foresight is tormented by hypochondria while his wife is seduced before his face. But if this is not Lamb's 'Utopia of gallantry', it is nonetheless the make-believe world of the theatre. If the audience will not laugh at *this*, it is doubtful if the Catos of the pit will laugh at anything. It is, of

[15] E. T. Norris 'A Possible Origin of Congreve's Sailor Ben', *Modern Language Notes* XLIX (1934), 334–5.
[16] Although Congreve may have had a rational contempt for astrology (he was involved in the famous Bickerstaff hoax), it is possible that Foresight was only intended as a satire on false astrology. Many of the leading figures of the day were interested in astrology, and William Lilly, whom Congreve mentions, was patronised by the Court.

course, very simple fare to offer to readers nourished by the complexities of modern academic analysis. So too is Ben's wooing of Miss Prue as through a loud hailer across the room; or, in Mozart, Leporello wooing Donna Elvira in the guise of Don Giovanni; or, in Shakespeare, Bottom with the head of an ass, loved by Titania. Sometimes one wonders whether, if we are not prepared to be like children, we should stay away from the theatre altogether. If *Love for Love* occasionally seems to impinge on serious matters, it returns swiftly to the world of fantasy again. Here, for instance, is Foresight sounding almost as if he were really angry:

> I defy you, hussy! But I'll remember this, I'll be revenged on you, cockatrice; I'll hamper you.—You have your fortune in your own hands, but I'll find a way to make your lover, your prodigal spendthrift gallant, Valentine, pay for all, I will. (II, 99–102)

But it is thus that Angelica rejoins:

> Will you? I care not, but all shall out then.—Look to it, nurse; I can bring witness you have a great unnatural teat under your left arm, and he another; and that you suckle a young devil in the shape of a tabby-cat by turns; I can.

This is high fantastical. It explodes at once into farce as nurse is overwhelmed:

> A teat, a teat, I an unnatural teat! O the false slanderous thing! Feel, feel here, if I have anything but like another Christian (*Crying*) or any teats but two that han't given suck this thirty years. (II,108–11)

It is, of course, the stage weeping of the nurse that provides the comic climax to the exchange.

Even the most serious of ethical poets have observed that it is pleasant to play the fool on occasion, and this is what Angelica is doing, and Congreve, and, one hopes, the audience. It is this low epicureanism which the high seriousness of Puritanical morality cannot stomach, this flippant Cavalier sophistication which while it persists in enjoying art with the naive acceptance of a child, insists on seeing it as a game. Foresight's anger is a stage anger. Nor, later, will he be a cuckold, because he is *not* married to Mrs. Foresight. Miss Prue has only a stage maidenhead to lose to sweet Mr. Tattle of about as much substance as the fair form of the amorous Titania. Even in the more corrupt world of *Don Giovanni*, no one credits that the hero goes to hell. Why else, by a self quotation, should Mozart remind us before the splendid horrors of the talking statue, that this is just another of his operas? Like all magic arts, the theatre belongs to charlatans.

But there is more to Congreve than polish, stage-craft, and high fantasy. Those who have admired him have sometimes called him a poet, not only for his care and refinement in the handling of language, but because there are in the plays suggestions of more general meaning beyond the local comic situation, and which carry one from the humour of situation and dialogue towards deeper, and sadder, concerns. The overtones are there in Foresight's speech first quoted: 'Methinks I look with a serene and benign aspect—pale, a little pale—but the roses of these cheeks have been gathered many years', or in the conclusion of the nurse's outburst, 'Feel, feel here, if I have anything but like another Christian or any teats but two that han't given suck this thirty years.' At another time, in a different place, this would not move laughter. It is the voice of pathos from behind the comic mask. We find it in Pope, or Mozart, or Watteau, whose Harlequin, Columbine, and Clown, Pater wrote, like tragedians in motley, are able 'to throw a world of serious innuendo into their burlesque looks, with a sort of comedy which shall be but tragedy seen from the other side.'[17] Yet, equally characteristic of Congreve, is the melancholy voice of disenchantment; for instance, Angelica's, 'Security is an insipid thing, and the overtaking and possessing of a wish discovers the folly of the chase. Never let us know one another better; for the pleasure of a masquerade is done when we come to show faces.' It could be a comment on Watteau, and it is coming close to the tragi-comedy of *The Way of the World*. It is no more than an element in the texture of the comedy, but it runs throughout. Here, for instance, is Valentine on Angelica (or Harlequin on Columbine, the names are indifferent):

> You're a woman, one to whom heaven gave beauty when it grafted roses on a briar. You are the reflection of heaven in a pond, and he that leaps at you is sunk. You are all white, a sheet of lovely spotless paper, when you first are born; but you are to be scrawled and blotted by every goose's quill. I know you; for I loved a woman, and loved her so long that I found out a strange thing: I found out what a woman was good for.
>
> TATTLE
> Aye, prithee, what's that?
> VALENTINE
> Why, to keep a secret.   (IV, 550–59)

The honied cadences of this bitter-sweet cynicism are obvious and even facile, but the total effect is not easy to describe, for the final bathetic fall, suspended over Tattle's interjection—one is tempted to use a musical analogy—seems like an evasion. Whatever it is that

[17] *Imaginary Portraits* (4th edn., London 1901), p. 6.

Valentine is thinking, the intrusion of Tattle leads him to repress. There is something that he avoids, but what it is remains a mystery. This is characteristic of Congreve. His comedy is, as it were, suspended. One move more and we might actually feel the texture of life, but then, whatever we would have, it would not be comedy. His art is a deliberate flirtation with experience, and its triumph is to tantalise with the appearance of life while denying the substance. In this he is like James, but is closer to what Pater called the 'marvellous tact of omission' in Watteau. There might be more than the game and the dance if Congreve did not cling to his style like a mask.

Whether this is maturity or mere frivolity, the kind of achievement we should admire in comic art, or a shirking of moral responsibility, probably only taste can decide. Perhaps, judged by the mature standard of those who use James as a measure of what is dull and trivial, Congreve is wanting, although judged by the mature standard of a Millamant, Isabel Archer sometimes appears little more than a goose. Nonetheless, those for whom art is a moral medicine should probably stay away from Congreve. Yet, first of all, one must have art. Congreve deserves to be judged by his best, a compliment hostile criticism has not always paid him. Therefore, in conclusion, perhaps taste may decide between two quotations, one from the climactic work of the Augustan playwright, the other from an artist undoubtedly more serious and morally profound in intention. But to which does the balance of aesthetic satisfaction incline?

MILLAMANT
   Come, don't look grave then. Well, what do you say to me?
MIRABELL
   I say that a man may as soon make a friend by his wit, or a fortune by his honesty, as win a woman with plain-dealing and sincerity.
MILLAMANT
   Sententious Mirabell! Prithee don't look with that violent and inflexible wise face, like Solomon at the dividing of the child in an old tapestry hanging.
MIRABELL
   You are merry, madam, but I would persuade you for a moment to be serious.
MILLAMANT
   What, with that face? No, if you keep your countenance, 'tis impossible I should hold mine. Well, after all, there is something very moving in a lovesick face. Ha, ha, ha—Well I won't laugh, don't be peevish—Heigho! Now I'll be melancholy, as melancholy as a watch-light. Well, Mirabell, if ever you will win me woo me now—Nay, if you are so tedious fare you well.
                                   (*The Way of the World*, II. v)

· · · · · · · · · ·

She had thought there was no source deeper than the phallic source. And now, behold, from the smitten rock of the man's body, from the strange marvellous flanks and thighs, deeper, further in mystery than the phallic source, came the floods of ineffable darkness and ineffable riches.

They were glad, and could forget perfectly. They laughed and went to the meal provided. There was a venison pasty, of all things, a large broad-faced cut ham, eggs and cresses and red beetroot, and medlars and apple-tart, and tea.

'What good things!' she cried with pleasure. 'How noble it looks! —shall I pour out the tea?'

(Women in Love, ch. 23.)

NOTE ON THE TEXT

Love for Love was first printed by Jacob Tonson in 1695. The present text is based upon this first quarto (Q1), and the copy text is from the Bodleian Library (Vet A 3e 112). There were three further editions in the same year, only one of which was acknowledged as the second edition (Q2). The third edition is dated 1697 (Q3), and the fourth 1704 (Q4). Congreve made a few minor revisions in these. For the collected edition of the *Works*, 1710 (W1), the text, in common with that of all his other plays, was extensively revised, partly to improve the sense and the grammar, partly to prune the play of licentious expressions. Acts were divided into scenes in the French fashion (on the entry or exit of a character). Three further editions of the *Works* appeared in Congreve's lifetime. The edition of 1719 (W2) claimed to incorporate further revisions, but these, as far as *Love for Love* is concerned, are very slight.

The present text is modernised in spelling, and the punctuation is a normalised version of the original. I have tried to preserve Congreve's rhetorical patterns while clarifying the syntax, rather than punctuate strictly according to modern conventions. The apparatus contains only substantive variants; punctuation, variant spellings, and contractions have been omitted. The scene divisions of the *Works* are recorded in square brackets in the text, but variants in the wording of stage directions between the first four quartos and the *Works* are not recorded unless they directly affect the movements of the actor, and I have permitted myself some unacknowledged normalisations.

FURTHER READING

Horace Walpole, 'Thoughts on Comedy' in *Works*, II, 1798.

William Hazlitt, *Lectures on the English Comic Writers* (1819).

Charles Lamb, 'On the Artificial Comedy of the Last Age' in *The Essays of Elia* (1821).

T. B. Macaulay, 'The Dramatic Works of Wycherley, Congreve, Vanbrugh and Farquhar', *Edinburgh Review* LXXII, 1841.

B. Dobrée, *Restoration Comedy* (Oxford, 1924).

K. M. Lynch, *The Social Mode of Restoration Comedy* (New York, 1926).

Virginia Woolf, 'Congreve's Comedies' in *The Moment* (1947).

T. H. Fujimura, *The Restoration Comedy of Wit* (Princeton, 1952).

N. N. Holland, *The First Modern Comedies* (Cambridge, Mass., 1959).

ed. J. Loftis, *Restoration Drama. Modern Essays in Criticism* (Galaxy Books, New York, 1966).

LOVE for LOVE:

A

COMEDY.

Acted at the

THEATRE in *Little Lincolns-Inn Fields*,

B Y

His Majesty's Servants.

Written by Mr. *CONGREVE.*

Nudus agris, nudus nummis paternis,
Insanire parat certa ratione modoque. Hor.

L O N D O N:

Printed for *Jacob Tonson*, at the *Judge's-Head*, near the
Inner-Temple-Gate in *Fleetstreet*. 1695.

Motto. Horace II *Sat.* iii 184 and 271 (reading *paret* not *parat*):
stripped of his lands and paternal wealth he prepares to go mad
by regular system and method

To the Right Honourable Charles Earl of Dorset and
Middlesex, Lord Chamberlain of His Majesty's Household,
and Knight of the Most Noble Order of the Garter, &c.

MY LORD,

A young poet is liable to the same vanity and indiscretion 5
with a young lover; and the great man that smiles upon one,
and the fine woman that looks kindly upon t'other, are each of
'em in danger of having the favour published with the first
opportunity.

But there may be a different motive, which will a little 10
distinguish the offenders. For though one should have a vanity
in ruining another's reputation, yet the other may only have an
ambition to advance his own. And I beg leave, my Lord, that I
may plead the latter, both as the cause and excuse of this
dedication. 15

Whoever is king, is also the father of his country; and as
nobody can dispute your Lordship's monarchy in poetry, so all
that are concerned ought to acknowledge your universal
patronage: and it is only presuming on the privilege of a loyal
subject that I have ventured to make this my address of thanks 20
to your Lordship; which, at the same time, includes a prayer
for your protection.

I am not ignorant of the common form of poetical dedica-
tions, which are generally made up of panegyrics, where the
authors endeavour to distinguish their patrons, by the shining 25
characters they give them, above other men. But that, my Lord,
is not my business at this time, nor is your Lordship *now* to be
distinguished. I am contented with the honour I do myself in
this epistle, without the vanity of attempting to add to, or
explain, your Lordship's character. 30

I confess it is not without some struggling that I behave
myself in this case as I ought: for it is very hard to be pleased
with a subject, and yet forbear it. But I choose rather to follow
Pliny's precept than his example, when in his panegyric to the
Emperor Trajan, he says, 35

---

6 *that smiles* (who smiles Ww)   7 *that looks* (who looks Ww)
7 *are each of* (are both of Ww)

1–2 *Charles . . . Middlesex*. (1638–1706). As Lord Chamberlain he was
    instrumental in the licensing of the Lincoln's Inn Theatre which
    opened with this play. He was a patron of Dryden and many others.

Nec minus considerabo quid aures ejus pati possint,
Quam quid virtutibus debeatur.

I hope I may be excused the pedantry of a quotation when it is so justly applied. Here are some lines in the print (and which your Lordship read before this play was acted) that were 40
omitted on the stage; and particularly one whole scene in the third act, which not only helps the design forward with less precipitation, but also heightens the ridiculous character of Foresight, which indeed seems to be maimed without it. But I found myself in great danger of a long play, and was glad to 45
help it where I could. Though notwithstanding my care, and the kind reception it had from the town, I could heartily wish it yet shorter: but the number of different characters represented in it would have been too much crowded in less room.

This reflection on prolixity (a fault for which scarce any one 50
beauty will atone) warns me not to be tedious now and detain your Lordship any longer with the trifles of,

MY LORD,

Your Lordship's
Most Obedient 55
and Most Humble
Servant,

WILL. CONGREVE

36–7 *Nec minus . . . debeatur* I will consider what he can tolerate to hear no less than what is due to his virtues
58 *WILL* (William Ww)

41–2 *scene in the third act.* Probably III. xi (in the edition of 1710).

A
PROLOGUE
FOR
The opening of the new Play-House, proposed to be spoken by
Mrs. Bracegirdle in man's clothes.

Sent from an unknown hand.

Custom, which everywhere bears mighty sway,
Brings me to act the orator today:
But women, you will say, are ill at speeches—
'Tis true, and therefore I appear in breeches:
Not for example to you City-wives;   5
That by prescription's settled for your lives.
Was it for gain the husband first consented?
O yes, their gains are mightily augmented:
  Making horns with her hands over her head
And yet, methinks, it must have cost some strife:
A passive husband, and an active wife!   10
'Tis awkward, very awkward, by my life.
But to my speech—assemblies of all nations
Still are supposed to open with orations:
Mine shall begin, to show our obligations.
To you, our benefactors, lowly bowing,   15
Whose favours have prevented our undoing;
A long Egyptian bondage we endured,
Till freedom by your justice we procured:
Our taskmasters were grown such very Jews,
We must at length have played in wooden shoes,   20
Had not your bounty taught us to refuse.
Freedom's of English growth, I think, alone;
What for lost English freedom can atone?
A free-born player loathes to be compelled;
Our rulers tyrannized, and we rebelled.   25
Freedom! the wise man's wish, the poor man's wealth;
Which you, and I, and most of us enjoy by stealth;
The soul of pleasure, and the sweet of life,
The woman's charter, widow, maid, or wife,
This they'd have cancelled, and thence grew the strife.   30
But you perhaps would have me here confess
How we obtained the favour—can't you guess?

  Prologue this prologue is om. in Ww

Why then I'll tell you (for I hate a lie),
By brib'ry, arrant brib'ry, let me die:
I was their agent, but by Jove I swear   35
No honourable member had a share,
Though young and able members bid me fair:
I chose a wiser way to make you willing,
Which has not cost the house a single shilling;
Now you suspect at least I went a-billing.   40
You see I'm young, and to that air of youth,
Some will add beauty, and a little truth;
These pow'rful charms, improved by pow'rful arts,
Prevailed to captivate your opening hearts.
Thus furnished, I preferred my poor petition,   45
And bribed ye to commiserate our condition:
I laughed, and sighed, and sung, and leered upon ye;
With roguish loving looks, and that way won ye:
The young men kissed me, and the old I kissed,
And luringly I led them as I list.   50
The ladies in mere pity took our parts,
Pity's the darling passion of their hearts.
Thus bribing, or thus bribed, fear no disgraces:
For thus you may take bribes, and keep your places.

PROLOGUE

Spoken at the opening of the New House,
By Mr. Betterton

The husbandman in vain renews his toil,
To cultivate each year a hungry soil;
And fondly hopes for rich and generous fruit,
When what should feed the tree, devours the root:
Th'unladen boughs, he sees, bode certain dearth,   5
Unless transplanted to more kindly earth.
So, the poor husbands of the stage, who found
Their labours lost upon the ungrateful ground,
This last and only remedy have proved;
And hope new fruit from ancient stocks removed.   10
Well may they hope, when you so kindly aid,
And plant a soil which you so rich have made.
As Nature gave the world to man's first age,
So from your bounty we receive this stage;
The freedom man was born to, you've restored,   15
And to our world such plenty you afford,
It seems like Eden, fruitful of its own accord.
But since in Paradise frail flesh gave way,
And when but two were made, both went astray;
Forbear your wonder, and the fault forgive,   20
If in our larger family we grieve
One falling Adam, and one tempted Eve;
We who remain would gratefully repay
What our endeavours can, and bring this day,
The first-fruit offering of a virgin play.   25
We hope there's something that may please each taste,
And though of homely fare we make the feast,
Yet you will find variety at least.
There's humour, which for cheerful friends we got,
And for the thinking party there's a plot.   30
We've something too, to gratify ill nature
(If there be any here) and that is Satire—

8 *upon the* (upon Ww)
12 *And plant* (plant Ww)

---

22 *Adam . . . Eve*. Joseph Williams and Susanna Mountfort, both of
whom had seceded from Lincoln's Inn Fields to the 'taskmasters' of
the rival company.

7

Though Satire scarce dares grin, 'tis grown so mild;
Or only shows its teeth, as if it smiled.
As asses thistles, poets mumble wit,   35
And dare not bite, for fear of being bit.
They hold their pens, as swords are held by fools,
And are afraid to use their own edge-tools.
Since the *Plain Dealer*'s scenes of manly rage,
Not one has dared to lash this crying age.   40
This time the poet owns the bold essay,
Yet hopes there's no ill manners in his play:
And he declares by me, he has designed
Affront to none, but frankly speaks his mind.
And should th'ensuing scenes not chance to hit,   45
He offers but this one excuse: 'twas writ
Before your late encouragement of wit.

39 *Plain Dealer's . . . rage.* Wycherley's play (1676). The misanthropic
hero is called Manly. Congreve is paying lip-service to the 17th-
century belief that satire should lash vice (as Wycherley and Juvenal
had done), but his manner is closer to the polite ridicule of Horace.
Times were changing.

[Dramatis Personae]

Men

SIR SAMPSON LEGEND, *father to Valentine and Ben*	Mr. Underhill
VALENTINE, *fallen under his father's displeasure by his expensive way of living, in love with Angelica*	Mr. Betterton
SCANDAL, *his friend, a free speaker*	Mr. Smith
TATTLE, *a half-witted beau, vain of his amours, yet valuing himself for secrecy*	Mr. Bowman
BEN, *Sir Sampson's younger son, half home-bred, and half sea-bred, designed to marry Miss Prue*	Mr. Dogget
FORESIGHT, *an illiterate old fellow, peevish and positive, superstitious, and pretending to understand astrology, palmistry, physiognomy, omens, dreams, etc., uncle to Angelica*	Mr. Sandford
JEREMY, *servant to Valentine*	Mr. Bowen
TRAPLAND, *a scrivener*	Mr. Triffusis
BUCKRAM, *a lawyer*	Mr. Freeman

Women

ANGELICA, *niece to Foresight, of a considerable fortune in her own hands*	Mrs. Bracegirdle
MRS. FORESIGHT, *second wife to Foresight*	Mrs. Bowman
MRS. FRAIL, *sister to Mrs. Foresight, a woman of the town*	Mrs. Barry
MISS PRUE, *daughter to Foresight by a former wife, a silly, awkward, country girl*	Mrs. Ayliff
NURSE *to Miss* [Prue]	Mrs. Leigh
JENNY, *maid to Angelica*	Mrs. Lawson

A STEWARD, OFFICERS, SAILORS, AND SEVERAL SERVANTS

The Scene: *in London*]

2 *Men* ed. (Men by Q1)
18 *Women* ed. (Women by Q1)
27 *maid to Angelica* (om. Ww)

9

LOVE FOR LOVE

[Act I, Scene i]

VALENTINE *in his chamber, reading.* JEREMY *waiting. Several*
books upon the table

VALENTINE

Jeremy.

JEREMY

Sir.

VALENTINE

Here, take away. I'll walk a turn and digest what I have read.

JEREMY (*Aside, and taking away the books*)

You'll grow devilish fat upon this paper diet.

VALENTINE

And d'ye hear, go you to breakfast. There's a page doubled   5
down in Epictetus that is a feast for an emperor.

JEREMY

Was Epictetus a real cook, or did he only write receipts?

VALENTINE

Read, read, sirrah, and refine your appetite; learn to live
upon instruction; feast your mind, and mortify your flesh;
read, and take your nourishment in at your eyes; shut up   10
your mouth, and chew the cud of understanding. So
Epictetus advises.

JEREMY

O Lord! I have heard much of him when I waited upon a
gentleman at Cambridge. Pray, what was that Epictetus?

VALENTINE

A very rich man—not worth a groat.   15

JEREMY

Humph, and so he has made a very fine feast, where there is
nothing to be eaten.

VALENTINE

Yes.

JEREMY

Sir, you're a gentleman, and probably understand this fine
feeding; but if you please, I had rather be at board-wages.   20
Does your Epictetus, or your Seneca here, or any of these

7 *receipts* recipes

poor rich rogues, teach you how to pay your debts without
money? Will they shut up the mouths of your creditors?
Will Plato be bail for you? Or Diogenes, because he under-
stands confinement and lived in a tub, go to prison for you?   25
S'life, sir, what do you mean, to mew yourself up here with
three or four musty books in commendation of starving and
poverty?

VALENTINE

Why, sirrah, I have no money, you know it; and therefore
resolve to rail at all that have: and in that I but follow the   30
examples of the wisest and wittiest men in all ages, these
poets and philosophers whom you naturally hate, for just
such another reason: because they abound in sense, and you
are a fool.

JEREMY

Aye, sir, I am a fool, I know it; and yet, heaven help me,   35
I'm poor enough to be a wit. But I was always a fool when I
told you what your expenses would bring you to; your
coaches and your liveries; your treats and your balls; your
being in love with a lady that did not care a farthing for you
in your prosperity; and keeping company with wits that   40
cared for nothing but your prosperity; and now when you
are poor, hate you as much as they do one another.

VALENTINE

Well, and now I am poor, I have an opportunity to be
revenged on 'em all; I'll pursue Angelica with more love
than ever, and appear more notoriously her admirer in this   45
restraint, than when I openly rivalled the rich fops that
made court to her; so shall my poverty be a mortification to
her pride and, perhaps, make her compassionate that love
which has principally reduced me to this lowness of fortune.
And for the wits, I'm sure I'm in a condition to be even   50
with them.

JEREMY

Nay, your condition is pretty even with theirs, that's the
truth on't.

VALENTINE

I'll take some of their trade out of their hands.

31–2 *men in all ages, these poets and* (om. Ww)
48 *that love* (the love Q3, 4, Ww)
50 *I'm sure I'm* (I'm sure I am Ww)

22 *poor rich rogues*. But Seneca was extremely wealthy. Jeremy's classical
   erudition has let him down?

JEREMY

Now heaven of mercy continue the tax upon paper; you   55
don't mean to write!

VALENTINE

Yes, I do; I'll write a play.

JEREMY

Hem! Sir, if you please to give me a small certificate of three
lines—only to certify those whom it may concern: that the
bearer hereof, Jeremy Fetch by name, has for the space of   60
seven years truly and faithfully served Valentine Legend
Esq.; and that he is not now turned away for any misde-
meanour; but does voluntarily dismiss his master from any
future authority over him—

VALENTINE

No, sirrah, you shall live with me still.   65

JEREMY

Sir, it's impossible—I may die with you, starve with you, or
be damned with your works; but to live even three days, the
life of a play, I no more expect it than to be canonized for a
Muse after my decease.

VALENTINE

You are witty, you rogue! I shall want your help. I'll have   70
you learn to make couplets, to tag the ends of acts, d'ye
hear, get the maids to Crambo in an evening, and learn the
knack of rhyming. You may arrive at the height of a song,
sent by an unknown hand, or a chocolate-house lampoon.

JEREMY

But, sir, is this the way to recover your father's favour?   75
Why, Sir Sampson will be irreconcilable. If your younger
brother should come from sea, he'd never look upon you
again. You're undone, sir; you're ruined; you won't have a
friend left in the world if you turn poet. Ah, pox confound
that Will's Coffee-House; it has ruined more young men   80
than the Royal Oak Lottery. Nothing thrives that belongs
to't. The man of the house would have been an alderman by
this time with half the trade if he had set up in the City.
For my part, I never sit at the door that I don't get double

72 *Crambo* capping verses

67-8 *three days . . . play*. The third night's proceeds were for the author's
'benefit'.
80 *Will's Coffee-House*. The resort of Congreve himself and other leading
literary figures.

the stomach that I do at a horse race. The air upon Banstead   85
Downs is nothing to it for a whetter; yet I never see it, but
the Spirit of Famine appears to me; sometimes like a decayed
porter, worn out with pimping and carrying *billet-doux* and
songs; not like other porters for hire, but for the jest's sake;
now like a thin chairman, melted down to half is proportion   90
with carrying a poet upon tick to visit some great fortune;
and his fare to be paid him like the wages of sin, either at the
day of marriage, or the day of death.

VALENTINE
Very well, sir; can you proceed?

JEREMY
Sometimes like a bilked bookseller, with a meagre terrified   95
countenance, that looks as if he had written for himself, or
were resolved to turn author and bring the rest of his
brethren into the same condition. And lastly, in the form of
a worn-out punk, with verses in her hand, which her vanity
had preferred to settlements, without a whole tatter to her   100
tail, but as ragged as one of the Muses; or as if she were
carrying her linen to the paper-mill, to be converted into
folio books, of warning to all young maids not to prefer
poetry to good sense; or lying in the arms of a needy wit,
before the embraces of a wealthy fool.   105

[Act I, Scene ii]

Enter SCANDAL

SCANDAL
What, Jeremy holding forth?

VALENTINE
The rogue has (with all the wit he could muster up) been
declaiming against wit.

SCANDAL
Aye? Why then I'm afraid Jeremy has wit; for wherever it
is, it's always contriving its own ruin.   110

JEREMY
Why, so I have been telling my master, sir. Mr. Scandal, for
heaven's sake, sir, try if you can dissuade him from turning
poet.

SCANDAL
Poet! He shall turn soldier first, and rather depend upon the

85-6 *Banstead Downs* a racecourse near Epsom
95 *bilked* cheated
99 *punk* prostitute

outside of his head than the lining. Why, what the devil, has 115
not your poverty made you enemies enough? Must you
needs show your wit to get more?

JEREMY

Aye, more indeed; for who cares for anybody that has more
wit than himself?

SCANDAL

Jeremy speaks like an oracle. Don't you see how worthless 120
great men, and dull rich rogues, avoid a witty man of small
fortune? Why, he looks like a writ of enquiry into their titles
and estates; and seems commissioned by heaven to seize the
better half.

VALENTINE

Therefore I would rail in my writings and be revenged. 125

SCANDAL

Rail? At whom? The whole world? Impotent and vain!
Who would die a martyr to sense in a country where the
religion is folly? You may stand at bay for awhile; but when
the full cry is against you, you won't have fair play for your
life. If you can't be fairly run down by the hounds, you will 130
be treacherously shot by the huntsmen. No, turn pimp,
flatterer, quack, lawyer, parson, be chaplain to an atheist, or
stallion to an old woman, anything but poet; a modern poet
is worse, more servile, timorous, and fawning, than any I
have named; without you could retrieve the ancient honours 135
of the name, recall the stage of Athens, and be allowed the
force of open honest satire.

VALENTINE

You are as inveterate against our poets as if your character
had been lately exposed upon the stage. Nay, I am not
violently bent upon the trade. (*One knocks*) Jeremy, see 140
who's there.   *Exit* JEREMY
But tell me what you would have me do? What do the world
say of me, and my forced confinement?

SCANDAL

The world behaves itself as it used to do on such occasions;
some pity you, and condemn your father; others excuse him, 145
and blame you; only the ladies are merciful and wish you
well, since love and pleasurable expense have been your
greatest faults.

129 *you won't* (you shan't Ww)
141 s.d. *Exit* JEREMY (JEREMY *goes to the door* Ww)
142 *What do* (What does Ww)   144 *used* (uses Ww)

Enter JEREMY

VALENTINE

How now?

JEREMY

Nothing new, sir; I have despatched some half a dozen duns   150
with as much dexterity as a hungry judge does causes at
dinner time.

VALENTINE

What answer have you given 'em?

SCANDAL

Patience, I suppose, the old receipt.

JEREMY

No, faith, sir; I have put 'em off so long with patience and   155
forbearance and other fair words, that I was forced now to
tell 'em in plain downright English—

VALENTINE

What?

JEREMY

That they should be paid.

VALENTINE

When?   160

JEREMY

Tomorrow.

VALENTINE

And how the devil do you mean to keep your word?

JEREMY

Keep it? Not at all; it has been so very much stretched that
I reckon it will break of course by tomorrow, and nobody be
surprised at the matter. (*Knocking*) Again! Sir, if you don't   165
like my negotiation, will you be pleased to answer these
yourself?

VALENTINE

See who they are.   *Exit* JEREMY

[Act I, Scene iii]

VALENTINE

By this, Scandal, you may see what it is to be great; Secre-
taries of State, Presidents of the Council, and generals of an   170
army lead just such a life as I do, have just such crowds of
visitants in a morning, all soliciting of past promises; which
are but a civiller sort of duns, that lay claim to voluntary
debts.

148 s.d. *Enter* JEREMY (om. Ww)
150 *duns* creditors, or their agents, demanding payment

SCANDAL
And you, like a true great man, having engaged their   175
attendance, and promised more than ever you intend to
perform, are more perplexed to find evasions than you would
be to invent the honest means of keeping your word, and
gratifying your creditors.

VALENTINE
Scandal, learn to spare your friends, and do not provoke   180
your enemies; this liberty of your tongue will one day bring
a confinement on your body, my friend.

[Act I, Scene iv]

Enter JEREMY

JEREMY
O, sir, there's Trapland the scrivener, with two suspicious
fellows like lawful pads, that would knock a man down with
pocket-tipstaves—and there's your father's steward, and   185
the nurse with one of your children from Twitnam.

VALENTINE
Pox on her, could she find no other time to fling my sins in
my face? Here, give her this (*Gives money*) and bid her
trouble me no more. [*To* SCANDAL] A thoughtless two-
handed whore, she knows my condition well enough and   190
might have overlaid the child a fortnight ago if she had had
any forecast in her.

SCANDAL
What, is it bouncing Margery and my godson?

JEREMY
Yes, sir.

SCANDAL
My blessing to the boy, with this token (*Gives money*) of my   195
love. And, d'ye hear, bid Margery put more flocks in her
bed, shift twice a week, and not work so hard, that she may
not smell so vigorously.—I shall take the air shortly.

---

176 *intend* (intended Ww)
183 *scrivener* one who receives money of others to lay it out at interest
184 *lawful pads* not thieves (footpads) but bailiffs or constables
185 *tipstaves* metal-headed bludgeons
186 *Twitnam* Twickenham
191 *overlaid* smothered
193 *and my* (with my Ww)

VALENTINE

Scandal, don't spoil my boy's milk! [*To* JEREMY] Bid
Trapland come in.   *Exit* JEREMY   200
If I can give that Cerberus a sop, I shall be at rest for one
day.

[Act I, Scene v]

Enter TRAPLAND *and* JEREMY

VALENTINE

O Mr. Trapland! My old friend! Welcome. Jeremy, a chair
quickly; a bottle of sack and a toast—fly—a chair first.

TRAPLAND

A good morning to you, Mr. Valentine, and to you, Mr.   205
Scandal.

SCANDAL

The morning's a very good morning, if you don't spoil it.

VALENTINE

Come sit you down, you know his way.

TRAPLAND (*Sits*)

There is a debt, Mr. Valentine, of 1500 pounds of pretty
long standing—   210

VALENTINE

I cannot talk about business with a thirsty palate.—Sirrah,
the sack.

TRAPLAND

And I desire to know what course you have taken for the
payment?

VALENTINE

Faith and troth, I am heartily glad to see you, my service to   215
you. [*To* JEREMY] Fill, fill, to honest Mr. Trapland, fuller.

TRAPLAND

Hold, sweetheart. This is not to our business—my service to
you, Mr. Scandal. (*Drinks*) I have forborne as long—

VALENTINE

T'other glass, and then we'll talk. Fill, Jeremy.

TRAPLAND

No more, in truth.—I have forborne, I say—   220

VALENTINE [*To* JEREMY]

Sirrah, fill when I bid you.—And how does your handsome
daughter? Come, a good husband to her!   *Drinks*

TRAPLAND

Thank you.—I have been out of this money—

204 *sack* a dry Spanish wine like sherry

VALENTINE
    Drink first. Scandal, why do you not drink?   *They drink*

TRAPLAND
    And in short, I can be put off no longer.   225

VALENTINE
    I was much obliged to you for your supply: it did me signal
service in my necessity. But you delight in doing good.—
Scandal, drink to me, my friend Trapland's health. An
honester man lives not, nor one more ready to serve his
friend in distress, though I say it to his face. Come, fill each   230
man his glass.

SCANDAL
    What, I know Trapland has been a whoremaster and loves a
wench still. You never knew a whoremaster that was not an
honest fellow.

TRAPLAND
    Fie, Mr. Scandal, you never knew—   235

SCANDAL
    What don't I know?—I know the buxom black widow in the
Poultry—800 pounds a year jointure, and 20,000 pounds in
money. Ahah, old Trap!

VALENTINE
    Say you so, i'faith! Come, we'll remember the widow;
I know whereabouts you are: come, to the widow!   240

TRAPLAND
    No more indeed.

VALENTINE
    What, the widow's health; give it him—off with it! (*They
drink*) A lovely girl, i'faith, black sparkling eyes, soft pouting
ruby lips! Better sealing there than a bond for a million,
hah!   245

TRAPLAND
    No, no, there's no such thing; we'd better mind our
business—you're a wag.

VALENTINE
    No, faith, we'll mind the widow's business. Fill again.
Pretty round heaving breasts, a Barbary shape, and a jut with
her bum would stir an anchorite; and the prettiest foot! O, 250
if a man could but fasten his eyes to her feet, as they steal

236-7 *the Poultry* a street at the business end of London, east of
    Cheapside
237 *jointure* property settled on a woman at marriage to be enjoyed
    after her husband's death
249 *Barbary* Moorish; graceful in shape like an Arab steed

in and out, and play at Bo-peep under her petticoats, ah, Mr. Trapland?

TRAPLAND

Verily, give me a glass—you're a wag—and here's to the widow. *Drinks* 255

SCANDAL

He begins to chuckle; ply him close, or he'll relapse into a dun.

[Act I, Scene vi]

Enter OFFICER

OFFICER

By your leave, gentlemen—Mr. Trapland, if we must do our office, tell us. We have half a dozen gentlemen to arrest in Pall Mall and Covent Garden; and if we don't make haste 260 the chairmen will be abroad and block up the chocolate-houses, and then our labour's lost.

TRAPLAND

Udso, that's true. Mr. Valentine, I love mirth, but business must be done. Are you ready to—

JEREMY

Sir, your father's steward says he comes to make proposals 265 concerning your debts.

VALENTINE

Bid him come in. Mr. Trapland, send away your officer, you shall have an answer presently.

TRAPLAND

Mr. Snap, stay within call. *Exit* OFFICER

[Act I, Scene vii]

Enter STEWARD *and whispers* VALENTINE

SCANDAL

Here's a dog now, a traitor in his wine. [*To* TRAPLAND] 270 Sirrah, refund the sack: Jeremy, fetch him some warm water, or I'll rip up his stomach and go the shortest way to his conscience.

TRAPLAND

Mr. Scandal, you are uncivil; I did not value your sack; but you cannot expect it again when I have drank it. 275

269 s.d. *Enter* STEWARD *and whispers* (*Enter* STEWARD *who whispers* Ww)
275 *drank* (drunk Ww)

SCANDAL

And how do you expect to have your money again when a
gentleman has spent it?

VALENTINE [*To* STEWARD]

You need say no more, I understand the conditions; they are
very hard, but my necessity is very pressing: I agree to 'em.
Take Mr. Trapland with you, and let him draw the writing.   280
Mr. Trapland, you know this man; he shall satisfy you.

TRAPLAND

Sincerely, I am loath to be thus pressing, but my necessity—

VALENTINE

No apology, good Mr. Scrivener; you shall be paid.

TRAPLAND

I hope you forgive me, my business requires—

> *Exeunt* STEWARD, TRAPLAND *and* JEREMY

[Act I, Scene viii]

SCANDAL

He begs pardon like a hangman at an execution.   285

VALENTINE

But I have got a reprieve.

SCANDAL

I am surprised; what, does your father relent?

VALENTINE

No; he has sent me the hardest conditions in the world: you
have heard of a booby brother of mine that was sent to sea
three years ago? This brother, my father hears, is landed;   290
whereupon he very affectionately sends me word, if I will
make a deed of conveyance of my right to his estate after his
death to my younger brother, he will immediately furnish
me with four thousand pound to pay my debts, and make
my fortune. This was once proposed before, and I refused it;   295
but the present impatience of my creditors for their money,
and my own impatience of confinement and absence from
Angelica, force me to consent.

SCANDAL

A very desperate demonstration of your love to Angelica;
and I think she has never given you any assurance of hers.   300

VALENTINE

You know her temper; she never gave me any great reason
either for hope or despair.

SCANDAL

Women of her airy temper, as they seldom think before they

act, so they rarely give us any light to guess at what they mean: but you have little reason to believe that a woman of 305 this age, who has had an indifference for you in your prosperity, will fall in love with your ill fortune; besides, Angelica has a great fortune of her own; and great fortunes either expect another great fortune, or a fool.

[Act I, Scene ix]

Enter JEREMY

JEREMY

More misfortunes, sir. 310

VALENTINE

What, another dun?

JEREMY

No, sir, but Mr. Tattle is come to wait upon you.

VALENTINE

Well, I can't help it,—you must bring him up; he knows I don't go abroad. *Exit* JEREMY

[Act I, Scene x]

SCANDAL

Pox on him, I'll be gone. 315

VALENTINE

No, prithee stay: Tattle and you should never be asunder; you are light and shadow, and show one another; he is perfectly thy reverse both in humour and understanding; and as you set up for defamation, he is a mender of reputations.

SCANDAL

A mender of reputations! Aye, just as he is a keeper of 320 secrets, another virtue that he sets up for in the same manner. For the rogue will speak aloud in the posture of a whisper; and deny a woman's name, while he gives you the marks of her person. He will forswear receiving a letter from her, and at the same time show you her hand upon the superscription; 325 and yet perhaps he has counterfeited the hand too; and sworn to a truth, but he hopes not to be believed; and refuses the reputation of a lady's favour, as a doctor says, no, to a bishopric, only that it may be granted him. In short, he is a public professor of secrecy, and makes proclamation 330 that he holds private intelligence.—He's here.

325 *upon the* (in the Ww)

[Act I, Scene xi]

Enter TATTLE

TATTLE

Valentine, good morrow; Scandal, I am yours—that is, when you speak well of me.

SCANDAL

That is, when I am yours; for while I am my own, or anybody's else, that will never happen.   335

TATTLE

How inhuman!

VALENTINE

Why, Tattle, you need not be much concerned at anything that he says: for to converse with Scandal is to play at Losing Loadum; you must lose a good name to him before you can win it for yourself.   340

TATTLE

But how barbarous that is, and how unfortunate for him, that the world shall think the better of any person for his calumniation! I thank heaven, it has always been a part of my character to handle the reputation of others very tenderly.   345

SCANDAL

Aye, such rotten reputations as you have to deal with are to be handled tenderly indeed.

TATTLE

Nay, but why rotten? Why should you say rotten, when you know not the persons of whom you speak? How cruel that is!

SCANDAL

Not know 'em? Why, thou never hadst to do with anybody   350 that did not stink to all the town.

TATTLE

Ha, ha, ha! Nay, now you make a jest of it indeed. For there is nothing more known than that nobody knows anything of that nature of me: as I hope to be saved, Valentine, I never exposed a woman since I knew what woman was.   355

VALENTINE

And yet you have conversed with several.

338-9 *Losing Loadum* a card game in which the aim was to lose tricks
344 *reputation* (reputations Ww)
345 *tenderly* (tenderly indeed Ww)

TATTLE

　To be free with you, I have—I don't care if I own that. Nay, more (I'm going to say a bold word now), I never could meddle with a woman that had to do with anybody else.

SCANDAL

　How!   360

VALENTINE

　Nay, faith, I'm apt to believe him.—Except her husband, Tattle.

TATTLE

　O that—

SCANDAL

　What think you of that noble commoner, Mrs. Drab?

TATTLE

　Pooh, I know Madam Drab has made her brags in three or   365
four places that I said this and that, and writ to her, and did I know not what—but, upon my reputation, she did me wrong.—Well, well, that was malice, but I know the bottom of it. She was bribed to that by one that we all know—a man, too—only to bring me into disgrace with a certain woman   370
of quality—

SCANDAL

　Whom we all know.

TATTLE

　No matter for that.—Yes, yes, everybody knows, no doubt on't, everybody knows my secrets. But I soon satisfied the lady of my innocence; for I told her—madam, says I, there   375
are some persons who make it their business to tell stories, and say this and that of one and t'other, and everything in the world; and, says I, if your Grace—

SCANDAL

　Grace!

TATTLE

　O Lord, what have I said? My unlucky tongue!   380

VALENTINE

　Ha, ha, ha!

SCANDAL

　Why Tattle, thou hast more impudence than one can in reason expect: I shall have an esteem for thee. Well, and ha, ha, ha! well, go on, and what did you say to her Grace?

VALENTINE

　I confess this is something extraordinary.   385

369 *one that we* (one we Ww)

TATTLE

Not a word, as I hope to be saved, an arrant *lapsus linguae*—
come, let's talk of something else.

VALENTINE

Well, but how did you acquit yourself?

TATTLE

Pooh, pooh, nothing at all, I only rallied with you.—A
woman of ordinary rank was a little jealous of me, and I told 390
her something or other, faith—I know not what—come, let's
talk of something else.   *Hums a song*

SCANDAL

Hang him, let him alone; he has a mind we should inquire.

TATTLE

Valentine, I supped last night with your mistress, and her
uncle old Foresight. I think your father lies at Foresight's? 395

VALENTINE

Yes.

TATTLE

Upon my soul, Angelica's a fine woman—and so is Mrs.
Foresight, and her sister Mrs. Frail.

SCANDAL

Yes, Mrs. Frail is a very fine woman; we all know her.

TATTLE

O, that is not fair.   400

SCANDAL

What?

TATTLE

To tell.

SCANDAL

To tell what? Why, what do you know of Mrs. Frail?

TATTLE

Who, I? Upon honour I don't know whether she be man or
woman but by the smoothness of her chin and roundness of 405
her lips.

SCANDAL

No!

TATTLE

No.

SCANDAL

She says otherwise.

TATTLE

Impossible!   410

406 *lips* (hips Ww)

SCANDAL

Yes, faith. Ask Valentine else.

TATTLE

Why then, as I hope to be saved, I believe a woman only obliges a man to secrecy that she may have the pleasure of telling herself.

SCANDAL

No doubt on't. Well, but has she done you wrong, or no? 415 You have had her? Ha?

TATTLE

Though I have more honour than to tell first, I have more manners than to contradict what a lady has declared.

SCANDAL

Well, you own it?

TATTLE

I am strangely surprised! Yes, yes, I can't deny it, if she 420 taxes me with it.

SCANDAL

She'll be here by and by; she sees Valentine every morning.

TATTLE

How!

VALENTINE

She does me the favour—I mean of a visit sometimes. I did not think she had granted more to anybody. 425

SCANDAL

Nor I, faith—but Tattle does not use to belie a lady; it is contrary to his character.—How one may be deceived in a woman, Valentine!

TATTLE

Nay, what do you mean, gentlemen?

SCANDAL

I'm resolved I'll ask her. 430

TATTLE

O barbarous! Why did you not tell me—

SCANDAL

No, you told us.

TATTLE

And bid me ask Valentine?

VALENTINE

What did I say? I hope you won't bring me to confess an answer, when you never asked me the question. 435

TATTLE

But, gentlemen, this is the most inhuman proceeding—

VALENTINE

Nay, if you have known Scandal thus long, and cannot avoid
such a palpable decoy as this was, the ladies have a fine time
whose reputations are in your keeping.

[Act I, Scene xii]

Enter JEREMY

JEREMY

Sir, Mrs. Frail has sent to know if you are stirring. 440

VALENTINE

Show her up when she comes. *Exit* JEREMY

[Act I, Scene xiii]

TATTLE

I'll be gone.

VALENTINE

You'll meet her.

TATTLE

Have you not a back way?

VALENTINE

If there were, you have more discretion than to give Scandal 445
such an advantage; why, your running away will prove all
that he can tell her.

TATTLE

Scandal, you will not be so ungenerous.—O, I shall lose my
reputation of secrecy forever! I shall never be received but
upon public days, and my visits will never be admitted be- 450
yond a drawing room: I shall never see a bedchamber again,
never be locked in a closet, nor run behind a screen, or under
a table; never be distinguished among the waiting-women by
the name of trusty Mr. Tattle more.—You will not be so
cruel! 455

VALENTINE

Scandal, have pity on him; he'll yield to any conditions.

TATTLE

Any, any terms.

SCANDAL

Come then, sacrifice half a dozen women of good reputation
to me presently. Come, where are you familiar?—And see
that they are women of quality, too, the first quality. 460

444 *Have you* (Is there Ww)
459 *you* Ww (your Qq)

TATTLE

'Tis very hard. Won't a baronet's lady pass?

SCANDAL

No, nothing under a Right Honourable.

TATTLE

O inhuman! You don't expect their names?

SCANDAL

No, their titles shall serve.

TATTLE

Alas, that's the same thing. Pray spare me their titles; I'll   465
describe their persons.

SCANDAL

Well, begin then; but take notice, if you are so ill a painter
that I cannot know the person by your picture of her, you
must be condemned, like other bad painters, to write the
name at the bottom.   470

TATTLE

Well, first then—

[Act I, Scene xiv]

Enter MRS. FRAIL

TATTLE

O unfortunate! She's come already. Will you have patience
till another time—I'll double the number.

SCANDAL

Well, on that condition. Take heed you don't fail me.

MRS. FRAIL

Hey day! I shall get a fine reputation by coming to see   475
fellows in a morning. Scandal, you devil, are you here too?
O, Mr. Tattle, everything is safe with you we know.

SCANDAL

Tattle!

TATTLE

Mum.—O, madam, you do me too much honour.

VALENTINE

Well, Lady Galloper, how does Angelica?   480

MRS. FRAIL

Angelica? Manners!

VALENTINE

What, you will allow an absent lover—

475 *Hey day* (om. Ww)

MRS. FRAIL

No, I'll allow a lover present with his mistress to be particular, but otherwise I think his passion ought to give place to his manners.   485

VALENTINE

But what if he have more passion than manners?

MRS. FRAIL

Then let him marry and reform.

VALENTINE

Marriage indeed may qualify the fury of his passion, but it very rarely mends a man's manners.

MRS. FRAIL

You are the most mistaken in the world; there is no creature   490
perfectly civil but a husband. For in a little time he grows only rude to his wife, and that is the highest good breeding, for it begets his civility to other people. Well, I'll tell you news; but I suppose you hear your brother Benjamin is landed. And my brother Foresight's daughter is come out of   495
the country. I assure you, there's a match talked of by the old people. Well, if he be but as great a sea-beast as she is a land-monster, we shall have a most amphibious breed. The progeny will be all otters; he has been bred at sea, and she has never been out of the country.   500

VALENTINE

Pox take 'em, their conjunction bodes no good I'm sure.

MRS. FRAIL

Now you talk of conjunction, my brother Foresight has cast both their nativities, and prognosticates an admiral and an eminent justice of the peace to be the issue-male of their two bodies. 'Tis the most superstitious old fool! He would   505
have persuaded me that this was an unlucky day and would not let me come abroad: but I invented a dream and sent him to Artimedorus for interpretation, and so stole out to see you. Well, and what will you give me now? Come, I must have something.   510

---

486 *he have* (he has Ww)
501 *bodes no* Q1–2 (bodes me no Q3, 4, Ww)
502 *conjunction* the apparent proximity of two heavenly bodies; their sharing the same longitude
502 *has* (hast Q1 uncorr. cited by Davis)

---

508 *Artimedorus*. Soothsayer and interpreter of dreams (2nd century A.D.).

VALENTINE

Step into the next room—and I'll give you something.

SCANDAL

Aye, we'll all give you something.

MRS. FRAIL

Well, what will you all give me?

VALENTINE

Mine's a secret.

MRS. FRAIL

I thought you would give me something that would be a   515
trouble to you to keep.

VALENTINE

And Scandal shall give you a good name.

MRS. FRAIL

That's more than he has for himself. And what will you give
me, Mr. Tattle?

TATTLE

I? My soul, madam.   520

MRS. FRAIL

Pooh, no, I thank you, I have enough to do to take care of my
own. Well; but I'll come and see you one of these mornings:
I hear you have a great many pictures.

TATTLE

I have a pretty good collection at your service, some
originals.   525

SCANDAL

Hang him, he has nothing but the *Seasons* and the *Twelve
Caesars*, paltry copies; and the *Five Senses*, as ill represented
as they are in himself; and he himself is the only original
you will see there.

MRS. FRAIL

Aye, but I hear he has a closet of beauties.   530

SCANDAL

Yes, all that have done him favours, if you will believe him.

MRS. FRAIL

Aye, let me see those, Mr. Tattle.

TATTLE

O, madam, those are sacred to love and contemplation. No
man but the painter and myself was ever blest with the sight.

526–7 Prints of the paintings of Pierre Breughel le Jeune (Davis). The
    Twelve Caesars adorn the walls in Hogarth's *Rake's Progress*, III
    (Summers), and are ascribed to Titian.

MRS. FRAIL

Well, but a woman—　　　　　　　　　　　　　　　　535

TATTLE

Nor woman, till she consented to have her picture there too
—for then she is obliged to keep the secret.

SCANDAL

No, no; come to me if you would see pictures.

MRS. FRAIL

You?

SCANDAL

Yes, faith, I can show you your own picture and most of　540
your acquaintance to the life, and as like as at Kneller's.

MRS. FRAIL

O lying creature—Valentine, does not he lie? I can't believe
a word he says.

VALENTINE

No, indeed, he speaks truth now: for as Tattle has pictures
of all that have granted him favours, he has the pictures of　545
all that have refused him; if satires, descriptions, characters
and lampoons are pictures.

SCANDAL

Yes, mine are most in black and white. And yet there are
some set out in their true colours, both men and women. I
can show you pride, folly, affectation, wantonness, incon-　550
stancy, covetousness, dissimulation, malice and ignorance,
all in one piece. Then I can show you lying, foppery, vanity,
cowardice, bragging, lechery, impotence and ugliness in
another piece; and yet one of these is a celebrated beauty
and t'other a professed beau. I have paintings too, some　555
pleasant enough.

MRS. FRAIL

Come, let's hear 'em.

SCANDAL

Why, I have a beau in a bagnio, cupping for a complexion,
and sweating for a shape.

MRS. FRAIL

So.　　　　　　　　　　　　　　　　　　　　　　560

537 *she is* (she's Ww)
538 *you would* (you'd Ww)
558 *bagnio* bathing house
558 *cupping* being bled

541 *Kneller's*. Sir Godfrey Kneller (1646–1726), the fashionable and
prolific portrait painter. He painted the Kit-Cat Club portraits.

SCANDAL

Then I have a lady burning of brandy in a cellar with a
hackney-coachman.

MRS. FRAIL

O devil! Well, but that story is not true.

SCANDAL

I have some hieroglyphics too; I have a lawyer with a
hundred hands, two heads, and but one face; a divine with   565
two faces, and one head; and I have a soldier with his brains
in his belly, and his heart where his head should be.

MRS. FRAIL

And no head?

SCANDAL

No head.

MRS. FRAIL

Pooh, this is all invention. Have you ne'er a poet?   570

SCANDAL

Yes, I have a poet weighing words and selling praise for
praise, and a critic picking his pocket. I have another large
piece too, representing a school, where there are huge-
proportioned critics, with long wigs, laced coats, Steinkirk
cravats, and terrible faces; with cat-calls in their hands, and 575
hornbooks about their necks. I have many more of this kind,
very well painted, as you shall see.

MRS. FRAIL

Well, I'll come, if it be only to disprove you.

[Act I, Scene xv]

Enter JEREMY

JEREMY

Sir, here's the steward again from your father.

VALENTINE

I'll come to him.—Will you give me leave? I'll wait on you   580
again presently.

561 *burning of brandy* (burning brandy Ww)
574–5 *Steinkirk cravats* a carelessly tied neckcloth (as worn by French
  officers at the battle of Steinkirk, 1692)
575 *cat-calls* squeaking instruments used at the theatre to express
  disapproval
576 *hornbooks* first books for children consisting of a leaf of paper
  protected by a leaf of transparent horn
578 *be only to* (be but to Ww)

MRS. FRAIL

No, I'll be gone. Come, who squires me to the Exchange? I must call my sister Foresight there.

SCANDAL

I will; I have a mind to your sister.

MRS. FRAIL

Civil!   585

TATTLE

I will; because I have a tender for your ladyship.

MRS. FRAIL

That's somewhat the better reason, to my opinion.

SCANDAL

Well, if Tattle entertains you, I have the better opportunity to engage your sister.

VALENTINE

Tell Angelica I am about making hard conditions to come   590
abroad and be at liberty to see her.

SCANDAL

I'll give an account of you, and your proceedings. If indiscretion be a sign of love, you are the most a lover of anybody that I know: you fancy that parting with your estate will help you to your mistress. In my mind he is a thoughtless   595
adventurer,
Who hopes to purchase wealth, by selling land;
Or win a mistress, with a losing hand.   *Exeunt*

[Act II, Scene i]

A room in FORESIGHT'S *house*

[*Enter*] FORESIGHT *and* SERVANT

FORESIGHT

Hey day! What, are all the women of my family abroad? Is not my wife come home? Nor my sister, nor my daughter?

SERVANT

No, sir.

FORESIGHT

Mercy on us, what can be the meaning of it? Sure the moon is in all her fortitudes. Is my niece Angelica at home?   5

586 *tender* (tendre W2)
590 *making* (to make Q4)
    4–5 *moon . . . fortitudes* the inconstant moon exerts her greatest
    power

SERVANT

Yes, sir.

FORESIGHT

I believe you lie, sir.

SERVANT

Sir?

FORESIGHT

I say you lie, sir. It is impossible that anything should be
as I would have it; for I was born, sir, when the Crab was   10
ascending, and all my affairs go backward.

SERVANT

I can't tell indeed, sir.

FORESIGHT

No, I know you can't, sir: but I can tell, sir, and foretell, sir.

[Act II, Scene ii]

Enter NURSE

FORESIGHT

Nurse, where's your young mistress?

NURSE

Wee'st heart, I know not; they're none of 'em come home   15
yet: poor child, I warrant she's fond o'seeing the town—
marry, pray heaven they ha' given her any dinner.—Good
lack-a-day, ha, ha, ha, O strange; I'll vow and swear now, ha,
ha, ha, marry, and did you ever see the like!

FORESIGHT

Why, how now, what's the matter?   20

NURSE

Pray heaven send your worship good luck, marry and amen
with all my heart, for you have put on one stocking with
the wrong side outward.

FORESIGHT

Ha, how? Faith and troth, I'm glad of it! and so I have! That
may be good luck in troth, in troth it may, very good luck: 25
nay, I have had some omens; I got out of bed backwards
too this morning, without premeditation; pretty good that
too; but then I stumbled coming down stairs, and met a
weasel; bad omens those: some bad, some good, our lives
are chequered, mirth and sorrow, want and plenty, night   30
and day, make up our time, but in troth I am pleased at my

13 *tell, sir, and* (*tell and* Ww)
15 *Wee'st* Woe is the

stocking; very well pleased at my stocking.—O, here's my
niece!

Enter ANGELICA

[*To* SERVANT] Sirrah, go tell Sir Sampson Legend I'll wait
on him if he's at leisure.—'Tis now three o'clock, a very   35
good hour for business; Mercury governs this hour.

Exit SERVANT

[Act II, Scene iii]

ANGELICA

Is not it a good hour for pleasure, too? Uncle, pray lend me
your coach; mine's out of order.

FORESIGHT

What, would you be gadding too? Sure all females are mad
today. It is of evil portent and bodes mischief to the master   40
of a family. I remember an old prophecy written by
Messehalah the Arabian, and thus translated by a reverend
Buckinghamshire bard.

<blockquote>
When housewives all the house forsake,
And leave good man to brew and bake,   45
Withouten guile, then be it said,
That house doth stond upon its head;
And when the head is set in grond,
Ne marl, if it be fruitful fond.
</blockquote>

Fruitful, the head fruitful, that bodes horns; the fruit of the   50
head is horns.—Dear niece, stay at home—for by the head of
the house is meant the husband; the prophecy needs no
explanation.

ANGELICA

Well, but I can neither make you a cuckold, uncle, by going
abroad; nor secure you from being one, by staying at home.   55

---

36 *Mercury* the god of merchandise and eloquence
48–9 *grond . . . fond* ground . . . found
49 *Ne marl* no wonder

---

42 *Messehalah.* Called by William Lilly, *England's Propheticall Merline*
(1644) 'a learned Arabian', but usually referred to as a Jewish astrologer (*c.* 9th century A.D.). Congreve possessed a copy of Lilly (see
John C. Hodges, ed., *The Library of William Congreve*, New York;
New York Public Library, 1955, item no. 359) and drew most of the
names of his astrologers thence.
43 *Buckinghamshire bard.* John Mason (d.1694). He was a millenarian.

FORESIGHT

Yes, yes; while there's one woman left, the prophecy is not in full force.

ANGELICA

But my inclinations are in force; I have a mind to go abroad; and if you won't lend me your coach, I'll take a hackney or a chair and leave you to erect a scheme and find who's in   60
conjunction with your wife. Why don't you keep her at home, if you're jealous when she's abroad? You know my aunt is a little retrograde (as you call it) in her nature. Uncle, I'm afraid you are not lord of the ascendant, ha, ha, ha!

FORESIGHT

Well, Jill-flirt, you are very pert, and always ridiculing that   65
celestial science.

ANGELICA

Nay, uncle, don't be angry. If you are, I'll reap up all your false prophecies, ridiculous dreams and idle divinations. I'll swear you are a nuisance to the neighbourhood. What a bustle did you keep against the last invisible eclipse, laying   70
in provision, as 'twere for a siege? What a world of fire and candle, matches and tinderboxes did you purchase! One would have thought we were ever after to live underground, or at least making a voyage to Greenland to inhabit there all the dark season.   75

FORESIGHT

Why, you malapert slut—

ANGELICA

Will you lend me your coach, or I'll go on—nay, I'll declare how your prophesied Popery was coming, only because the butler had mislaid some of the apostle's spoons and thought they were lost. Away went religion and spoon-meat together.   80
Indeed, uncle, I'll indict you for a wizard.

60 *erect a scheme* calculate by astrology
62 *jealous when* (jealous of her when Ww)
70 *did* (hid Q1 uncorr. cited by Davis)
76 *malapert* saucy
79 *apostle's spoons* (apostle spoons Ww)
80 *spoon-meat* broth, soft food given to infants

---

58 *inclinations . . . force*, a play on inclination in its astronomical sense. She also puns on 'retrograde' (astrologically: moving westward relative to the fixed stars) and 'ascendant' (astrologically: referring to the easternmost star rising at one's birth which was supposed to exert a commanding influence over one's life), here a jibe at Foresight's impotence.

FORESIGHT

How, hussy! was there ever such a provoking minx?

NURSE

O merciful father, how she talks!

ANGELICA

Yes, I can make oath of your unlawful midnight practices;
you and the old nurse there—   85

NURSE

Marry, heaven defend! I at midnight practices—O Lord,
what's here to do? I in unlawful doings with my master's
worship! Why, did you ever hear the like now?—Sir, did
ever I do anything of your midnight concerns—but warm
your bed, and tuck you up, and set the candle, and your   90
tobacco-box, and your urinal by you, and now and then rub
the soles of your feet?—O Lord, I!

ANGELICA

Yes, I saw you together, through the keyhole of the closet,
one night, like Saul and the Witch of Endor, turning the
sieve and shears, and pricking your thumbs, to write poor   95
innocent servants' names in blood, about a little nutmeg-
grater, which she had forgot in the caudle-cup. Nay, I know
something worse, if I would speak of it—

FORESIGHT

I defy you, hussy! But I'll remember this, I'll be revenged on
you, cockatrice; I'll hamper you.—You have your fortune in   100
your own hands, but I'll find a way to make your lover, your
prodigal spendthrift gallant, Valentine, pay for all, I will.

ANGELICA

Will you? I care not, but all shall out then.—Look to it,
nurse; I can bring witness that you have a great unnatural
teat under your left arm, and he another; and that you   105
suckle a young devil in the shape of a tabby-cat by turns; I
can.

NURSE

A teat, a teat, I an unnatural teat! O the false slanderous
thing! Feel, feel here, if I have anything but like another

97 *caudle-cup* warm drink
100 *cockatrice* a serpent-like monster; a basilisk which killed by its
    glance
103 *to it* (to't Ww)

---

94 *Witch of Endor*. See I *Samuel* xxviii.
95 *sieve and shears*. A means of divination in which the sieve was held
   between the extended points of the shears. Possibly a bawdy allusion.

Christian (*Crying*) or any teats but two that han't given suck   110
this thirty years.

FORESIGHT

I will have patience, since it is the will of the stars I should be
thus tormented. This is the effect of the malicious conjunc-
tions and oppositions in the third house of my nativity;
there the curse of kindred was foretold.—But I will have my   115
doors locked up—I'll punish you, not a man shall enter my
house.

ANGELICA

Do, uncle, lock 'em up quickly before my aunt come home.
You'll have a letter for alimony tomorrow morning. But let
me be gone first, and then let no mankind come near the   120
house, but converse with spirits and the celestial signs, the
Bull, and the Ram, and the Goat. Bless me! There are a great
many horned beasts among the twelve signs, uncle. But
cuckolds go to heaven.

FORESIGHT

But there's but one Virgin among the twelve signs, spitfire,   125
but one Virgin.

ANGELICA

Nor there had not been that one, if she had had to do with
anything but astrologers, uncle. That makes my aunt go
abroad.

FORESIGHT

How? How? Is that the reason? Come, you know something;   130
tell me, and I'll forgive you; do, good niece. Come, you shall
have my coach and horses, faith and troth you shall. Does
my wife complain? Come, I know women tell one another.
She is young and sanguine, has a wanton hazel eye, and was
born under Gemini, which may incline her to society; she   135
has a mole upon her lip, with a moist palm, and an open
liberality on the mount of Venus.

ANGELICA

Ha, ha, ha!

FORESIGHT

Do you laugh? Well, gentlewoman, I'll—but come, be a good
girl, don't perplex your poor uncle, tell me—won't you   140
speak? Odd, I'll—

110–11 *or any teats . . . years* (om. Ww)
114 *oppositions* the situation of heavenly bodies 180° apart
114 *third house* the third division of the Zodiac relates to brethren

136–7 *a mole . . . Venus.* These were all signs of sensuality.

[Act II, Scene iv]

Enter SERVANT

SERVANT
  Sir Sampson is coming down to wait upon you.

ANGELICA
  Goodbye, uncle. [*To* SERVANT] Call me a chair. I'll find out
  my aunt, and tell her she must not come home.

  Exit ANGELICA *and* SERVANT

FORESIGHT
  I'm so perplexed and vexed, I am not fit to receive him; I   145
  shall scarce recover myself before the hour be past. Go,
  nurse, tell Sir Sampson I'm ready to wait on him.

NURSE
  Yes, sir.   *Exit* NURSE

FORESIGHT
  Well—why if I was born to be a cuckold, there's no more to
  be said—   150

[Act II, Scene v]

Enter SIR SAMPSON LEGEND *with a paper*

SIR SAMPSON
  Nor no more to be done, old boy; that's plain—Here 'tis, I
  have it in my hand, old Ptolemy; I'll make the ungracious
  prodigal know who begat him; I will, old Nostrodamus.
  What, I warrant my son thought nothing belonged to a father
  but forgiveness and affection; no authority, no correction,   155
  no arbitrary power; nothing to be done, but for him to
  offend, and me to pardon. I warrant you, if he danced till
  doomsday, he thought I was to pay the piper. Well, but here
  it is under black and white, *signatum*, *sigillatum*, and
  deliberatum; that as soon as my son Benjamin is arrived, he   160
  is to make over to him his right of inheritance. Where's my
  daughter that is to be?—Hah! old Merlin! Body o'me, I'm
  so glad I'm revenged on this undutiful rogue.

---

150 *said—* (said— he's here already. Ww)
159–60 *signatum . . . deliberatum* signed, sealed, decided

---

153 *Nostrodamus*. (1503–66) Physician to Charles IX. He published a
  book of rhymed prophecies called *Centuries*.
162 *Merlin*. Alluding to Merlin's feats of divination, and perhaps to the
  assistance he gave in the marriage of Uther and Igraine (from which
  Arthur was born).

FORESIGHT

Odso, let me see; let me see the paper.—Aye, faith and troth,
here 'tis, if it will but hold. I wish things were done and the   165
conveyance made. When was this signed, what hour? Odso,
you should have consulted me for the time. Well, but we'll
make haste—

SIR SAMPSON

Haste, aye, aye; haste enough. My son Ben will be in town
tonight. I have ordered my lawyer to draw up writings of   170
settlement and jointure. All shall be done tonight. No
matter for the time; prithee, brother Foresight, leave
superstition. Pox o'th' time; there's no time but the time
present, there's no more to be said of what's past, and all that
is to come will happen. If the sun shine by day and the stars   175
by night, why, we shall know one another's faces without
the help of a candle, and that's all the stars are good for.

FORESIGHT

How, how? Sir Sampson, that all? Give me leave to contradict you, and tell you, you are ignorant.

SIR SAMPSON

I tell you I am wise; and *sapiens dominabitur astris*; there's   180
Latin for you to prove it, and an argument to confound your
Ephemeris. Ignorant! I tell you, I have travelled, old Fircu,
and know the globe. I have seen the Antipodes, where the
sun rises at midnight, and sets at noonday.

FORESIGHT

But I tell you, I have travelled, and travelled in the celestial   185
spheres, know the signs and the planets, and their houses;
can judge of motions direct and retrograde, of sextiles,
quadrates, trines and oppositions, fiery trigons and
aquatical trigons; know whether life shall be long or short,
happy or unhappy, whether diseases are curable or incurable,   190
if journeys shall be prosperous, undertakings successful, or
goods stolen recovered, I know—

180 *sapiens dominabitur astris* the wise man will be ruled by the stars.
     The tag was attributed to Ptolemy (Davis)
182 *Ephemeris* almanac
182 *Fircu* familiar spirit?
187–8 *sextiles . . . oppositions* the aspect of two planets as seen from
     earth distant from each other by a sixth, a quarter, a third or half
     the circle of the Zodiac
188–9 *fiery trigons and aquatical trigons* a trigon is the conjunction of
     three signs of the Zodiac; the fiery trigon: Aries, Leo, Sagittarius;
     the aquatical: Cancer, Scorpio, Pisces

SIR SAMPSON

I know the length of the Emperor of China's foot, have
kissed the Great Mogul's slipper, and rid a-hunting upon
an elephant with the Cham of Tartary. Body o'me, I have   195
made a cuckold of a king, and the present Majesty of
Bantam is the issue of these loins.

FORESIGHT

I know when travellers lie or speak truth, when they don't
know it themselves.

SIR SAMPSON

I have known an astrologer made a cuckold in the twinkling   200
of a star, and seen a conjurer that could not keep the devil
out of his wife's circle.

FORESIGHT (*Aside*)

What, does he twit me with my wife too? I must be better
informed of this.—Do you mean my wife, Sir Sampson?
Though you made a cuckold of the King of Bantam, yet by   205
the body of the sun—

SIR SAMPSON

By the horns of the moon, you would say, Brother Capricorn.

FORESIGHT

Capricorn in your teeth, thou modern Mandeville; Ferdi-
nand Mendez Pinto was but a type of thee, thou liar of the
first magnitude. Take back your paper of inheritance; send   210
your son to sea again. I'll wed my daughter to an Egyptian
mummy, ere she shall incorporate with a contemner of
sciences and a defamer of virtue.

SIR SAMPSON

Body o'me, I have gone too far; I must not provoke honest
Albumazar.—An Egyptian mummy is an illustrious creature,   215
my trusty hieroglyphic, and may have significations of
futurity about him; odsbud, I would my son were an
Egyptian mummy for thy sake. What, thou art not angry

197 *Bantam* in Java
202 *wife's* Ww (wives Qq)
207 *Capricorn* the goat, i.e. cuckold

208–9 *Mandeville . . . Pinto*. Sir John Mandeville the supposed author of
the famous Travels (mid-14th century); Pinto (?1509–85) was a Portu-
guese traveller of greater veracity than Foresight believes.
215 *Albumazar*. A 9th-century Arabian astronomer and astrologer. Thomas
Tomkis' play *Albumazar* (1615), an adaptation from the Italian, had
been revived in 1668.

for a jest, my good Haly? I reverence the sun, moon and
stars with all my heart. What, I'll make thee a present of a 220
mummy: now I think on't, body o'me, I have a shoulder of
an Egyptian king that I purloined from one of the pyramids,
powdered with hieroglyphics; thou shalt have it sent home
to thy house, and make an entertainment for all the philomaths and students in physic and astrology in and about 225
London.

FORESIGHT

But what do you know of my wife, Sir Sampson?

SIR SAMPSON

Thy wife is a constellation of virtues; she's the moon, and
thou art the man in the moon: nay, she is more illustrious
than the moon, for she has her chastity without her 230
inconstancy. 'S'bud, I was but in jest.

[Act II, Scene vi]

Enter JEREMY

SIR SAMPSON

How now, who sent for you? Ha! what would you have?

FORESIGHT

Nay, if you were but in jest.—Who's that fellow? I don't like
his physiognomy.

SIR SAMPSON

My son, sir? What son, sir? My son Benjamin, hoh? 235

JEREMY

No, sir, Mr. Valentine, my master. 'Tis the first time he has
been abroad since his confinement, and he comes to pay his
duty to you.

SIR SAMPSON

Well, sir.

223 *sent home* (brought home Ww)
224–5 *philomaths* lovers of learning

219 *Haly*. Referred to by Lilly as Hally Rodboan, and mentioned in
Tomkis' *Albumazar*. He is Ali ibn Rudhwan, supposed author of a
commentary on the pseudo-Ptolemaic *Centiloquium*, and another on
Galen's *Ars Medica*.

[Act II, Scene vii]

Enter VALENTINE

JEREMY

He is here, sir.　　　　　　　　　　　　　　　　240

VALENTINE

Your blessing, sir.

SIR SAMPSON

You've had it already, sir: I think I sent it you today in a
bill of four thousand pound. A great deal of money, brother
Foresight.

FORESIGHT

Aye, indeed, Sir Sampson, a great deal of money for a young　245
man; I wonder what he can do with it!

SIR SAMPSON

Body o'me, so do I.—Hark ye, Valentine, if there is too
much, refund the superfluity; do'st hear, boy?

VALENTINE

Superfluity, sir; it will scarce pay my debts. I hope you will
have more indulgence than to oblige me to those hard　250
conditions which my necessity signed to.

SIR SAMPSON

Sir, how; I beseech you, what were you pleased to intimate
concerning indulgence?

VALENTINE

Why, sir, that you would not go to the extremity of the
conditions, but release me at least from some part.　　　255

SIR SAMPSON

O, sir, I understand you,—that's all, ha?

VALENTINE

Yes, sir, all that I presume to ask.—But what you, out of
fatherly fondness, will be pleased to add, shall be doubly
welcome.

SIR SAMPSON

No doubt of it, sweet sir, but your filial piety and my　260
fatherly fondness would fit like two tallies.—Here's a rogue,
brother Foresight, makes a bargain under hand and seal in
the morning, and would be released from it in the afternoon.
—Here's a rogue, dog, here's conscience and honesty; this is
your wit now, this is the morality of your wits! You are a wit,　265
and have been a beau, and may be a—why, sirrah, is it not
here under hand and seal? Can you deny it?

247 *is too* (be too Ww)

VALENTINE

Sir, I don't deny it.

SIR SAMPSON

Sirrah, you'll be hanged; I shall live to see you go up
Holborn Hill.—Has he not a rogue's face? Speak brother, 270
you understand physiognomy; a hanging look to me; of all
my boys the most unlike me; a has a damned Tyburn face,
without the benefit o'the clergy.

FORESIGHT

Hum, truly I don't care to discourage a young man; he has a
violent death in his face, but I hope no danger of hanging. 275

VALENTINE

Sir, is this usage for your son? For that old weather-headed
fool, I know how to laugh at him; but you, sir—

SIR SAMPSON

You, sir; and you, sir! Why, who are you, sir?

VALENTINE

Your son, sir.

SIR SAMPSON

That's more than I know, sir, and I believe not. 280

VALENTINE

Faith, I hope not.

SIR SAMPSON

What, would you have your mother a whore! Did you ever
hear the like! Did you ever hear the like! Body o'me—

VALENTINE

I would have an excuse for your barbarity and unnatural
usage. 285

SIR SAMPSON

Excuse! Impudence! Why, sirrah, mayn't I do what I
please? Are not you my slave? Did not I beget you? And
might not I have chosen whether I would have begot you or
no? Ouns, who are you? Whence came you? What brought
you into the world? How came you here, sir? Here, to stand 290
here, upon those two legs, and look erect with that audacious
face, hah? Answer me that? Did you come a volunteer into
the world? Or did I beat up for you with the lawful
authority of a parent, and press you to the service?

VALENTINE

I know no more why I came, than you do why you called 295

272 *a has* (he has Q2–4, Ww)
293–4 *beat up for you . . . and* (om. Ww)

270 *Holborn Hill.* On the way from Newgate prison to Tyburn gallows.

me. But here I am, and if you don't mean to provide for me,
I desire you would leave me as you found me.

SIR SAMPSON

With all my heart: come, uncase, strip, and go naked out of
the world as you came into't.

VALENTINE

My clothes are soon put off; but you must also deprive me of   300
reason, thought, passions, inclinations, affections, appetites,
senses, and the huge train of attendants that you begot along
with me.

SIR SAMPSON

Body o'me, what a many-headed monster have I propagated!

VALENTINE

I am of myself, a plain easy simple creature, and to be kept   305
at small expense; but the retinue that you gave me are
craving and invincible; they are so many devils that you
have raised, and will have employment.

SIR SAMPSON

Ouns, what had I to do to get children? Can't a private man
be born without all these followers? Why, nothing under   310
an emperor should be born with appetites. Why, at this rate
a fellow that has but a groat in his pocket may have a stomach
capable of a ten-shilling ordinary.

JEREMY

Nay, that's as clear as the sun; I'll make oath of it before any
justice in Middlesex.   315

SIR SAMPSON

Here's a cormorant too.—'S'heart, this fellow was not born
with you? I did not beget him, did I?

JEREMY

By the provision that's made for me, you might have begot
me too: nay, and to tell your worship another truth, I
believe you did, for I find I was born with those same   320
whoreson appetites too, that my master speaks of.

SIR SAMPSON

Why, look you there now. I'll maintain it, that by the rule of
right reason, this fellow ought to have been born without a
palate. 'S'heart, what should he do with a distinguishing
taste? I warrant now he'd rather eat a pheasant than a piece   325
of poor John; and smell, now, why I warrant he can smell,

300 *deprive* (divest Ww)
313 *ordinary* eating house
316 *cormorant* glutton (the voracious seabird)
326 *poor John* dried or salted fish

and loves perfumes above a stink. Why, there's it, and
music—don't you love music, scoundrel?

JEREMY

Yes, I have a reasonable good ear, sir, as to jigs and country
dances, and the like; I don't much matter your solos or   330
sonatas; they give me the spleen.

SIR SAMPSON

The spleen, ha, ha, ha!—a pox confound you, solos and
sonatas? Ouns, whose son are you? How were you engen-
dered, muckworm?

JEREMY

I am, by my father, the son of a chairman; my mother sold   335
oysters in winter and cucumbers in summer; and I came
upstairs into the world, for I was born in a cellar.

FORESIGHT

By your looks, you should go upstairs out of the world too,
friend.

SIR SAMPSON

And if this rogue were anatomized now, and dissected, he   340
has his vessels of digestion and concoction, and so forth, large
enough for the inside of a cardinal, this son of a cucumber.
These things are unaccountable and unreasonable. Body
o'me, why was not I a bear, that my cubs might have lived
upon sucking their paws? Nature has been provident only to   345
bears and spiders; the one has its nutriment in his own
hands, and t'other spins his habitation out of his entrails.

VALENTINE

Fortune was provident enough to supply all the necessities
of my nature, if I had my right of inheritance.

SIR SAMPSON

Again! Ouns, han't you four thousand pound? If I had it   350
again, I would not give thee a groat. What, wouldst thou
have me turn pelican and feed thee out of my own vitals?
'S'heart, live by your wits. You were always fond of the wits,
now let's see if you have wit enough to keep yourself. Your
brother will be in town tonight, or tomorrow morning, and   355
then look you perform covenants, and so your friend and
servant.—Come, brother Foresight.

Exeunt SIR SAMPSON *and* FORESIGHT

347 *his entrails* (his own entrails Ww)

[Act II, Scene viii]

JEREMY
I told you what your visit would come to.

VALENTINE
'Tis as much as I expected. I did not come to see him: I came
to Angelica; but since she was gone abroad, it was easily   360
turned another way, and at least looked well on my side.—
What's here? Mrs. Foresight and Mrs. Frail; they are
earnest. I'll avoid 'em. Come this way, and go and inquire
when Angelica will return.   [*Exeunt*]

[Act II, Scene ix]

Enter MRS. FORESIGHT *and* MRS. FRAIL

MRS. FRAIL
What have you to do to watch me? S'life, I'll do what I   365
please.

MRS. FORESIGHT
You will?

MRS. FRAIL
Yes, marry will I. A great piece of business to go to Covent
Garden Square in a hackney-coach and take a turn with
one's friend.   370

MRS. FORESIGHT
Nay, two or three turns, I'll take my oath.

MRS. FRAIL
Well, what if I took twenty? I warrant if you had been there,
it had been only innocent recreation. Lord, where's the
comfort of this life, if we can't have the happiness of
conversing where we like?   375

MRS. FORESIGHT
But can't you converse at home? I own it, I think there's no
happiness like conversing with an agreeable man; I don't
quarrel at that, nor I don't think but your conversation was
very innocent; but the place is public, and to be seen with a
man in a hackney-coach is scandalous: what if anybody else   380
should have seen you alight as I did? How can anybody be
happy, while they're in perpetual fear of being seen and
censured? Besides, it would not only reflect upon you,
sister, but me.

MRS. FRAIL
Pooh, here's a clutter. Why should it reflect upon you? I   385

don't doubt but you have thought yourself happy in a
hackney-coach before now. If I had gone to Knightsbridge,
or to Chelsea, or to Spring-Garden, or Barn-Elms with a
man alone, something might have been said.

MRS. FORESIGHT

Why, was I ever in any of these places? What do you mean,   390
sister?

MRS. FRAIL

Was I? What do you mean?

MRS. FORESIGHT

You have been at a worse place.

MRS. FRAIL

I at a worse place, and with a man!

MRS. FORESIGHT

I suppose you would not go alone to the *World's-End*?   395

MRS. FRAIL

The world's end! What, do you mean to banter me?

MRS. FORESIGHT

Poor innocent! You don't know that there's a place called
the *World's-End*? I'll swear you can keep your countenance
purely; you'd make an admirable player.

MRS. FRAIL

I'll swear you have a great deal of impudence, and in my   400
mind too much for the stage.

MRS. FORESIGHT

Very well, that will appear who has most. You never were
at the *World's-End*?

MRS. FRAIL

No.

MRS. FORESIGHT

You deny it positively to my face?   405

MRS. FRAIL

Your face, what's your face?

MRS. FORESIGHT

No matter for that; it's as good a face as yours.

MRS. FRAIL

Not by a dozen years' wearing.—But I do deny it positively
to your face then.

390 *these* (those Ww)
400 *impudence* (confidence Ww)

---

395 *World's-End*. In Chelsea. All the places referred to were resorts of
doubtful character.

MRS. FORESIGHT

I'll allow you now to find fault with my face; for I'll swear   410
your impudence has put me out of countenance: but look you
here now—where did you lose this gold bodkin?—O, sister,
sister!

MRS. FRAIL

My bodkin!

MRS. FORESIGHT

Nay, 'tis yours, look at it.   415

MRS. FRAIL

Well, if you go to that, where did you find this bodkin? O,
sister, sister! Sister every way.

MRS. FORESIGHT (*Aside*)

O devil on't, that I could not discover her without betraying
myself.

MRS. FRAIL

I have heard gentlemen say, sister, that one should take great   420
care when one makes a thrust in fencing, not to lie open
one's self.

MRS. FORESIGHT

It's very true, sister: well, since all's out, and as you say,
since we are both wounded, let us do that is often done in
duels, take care of one another, and grow better friends than   425
before.

MRS. FRAIL

With all my heart. Ours are but slight flesh wounds, and if
we keep 'em from air, not at all dangerous: well, give me
your hand in token of sisterly secrecy and affection.

MRS. FORESIGHT

Here 'tis with all my heart.   430

MRS. FRAIL

Well, as an earnest of friendship and confidence, I'll acquaint
you with a design that I have: to tell truth and speak openly
one to another, I'm afraid the world have observed us more
than we have observed one another. You have a rich husband
and are provided for; I am at a loss and have no great stock   435
either of fortune or reputation, and therefore must look
sharply about me. Sir Sampson has a son that is expected
tonight, and by the account I have heard of his education,
can be no conjurer; the estate, you know, is to be made
over to him: now if I could wheedle him, sister, ha? You   440
understand me?

412 *bodkin* ornamental pin
424 *that* (what Ww)

MRS. FORESIGHT

I do; and will help you to the utmost of my power. And I
can tell you one thing that falls out luckily enough: my
awkward daughter-in-law, who you know is designed for his
wife, is grown fond of Mr. Tattle; now if we can improve that,　445
and make her have an aversion for the booby, it may go a
great way towards his liking of you. Here they come together;
and let us contrive some way or other to leave 'em together.

[Act II, Scene x]

Enter TATTLE *and* MISS PRUE

MISS PRUE

Mother, mother, mother, look you here.

MRS. FORESIGHT

Fie, fie, miss, how you bawl. Besides, I have told you, you　450
must not call me mother.

MISS PRUE

What must I call you then? Are not you my father's wife?

MRS. FORESIGHT

Madam; you must say, madam. By my soul, I shall fancy
myself old indeed, to have this great girl call me mother.
Well, but, miss, what are you so overjoyed at?　455

MISS PRUE

Look you here, madam, then, what Mr. Tattle has given me.
Look you here, cousin, here's a snuff-box; nay, there's snuff
in't;— here, will you have any?—O good! How sweet it is.—
Mr. Tattle is all over sweet, his peruke is sweet, and his
gloves are sweet, and his handkerchief is sweet, pure sweet,　460
sweeter than roses.—Smell him, mother, madam, I mean.
He gave me this ring for a kiss.

TATTLE

O fie, miss, you must not kiss and tell.

MISS PRUE

Yes; I may tell my mother.—And he says he'll give me
something to make me smell so.—O, pray lend me your　465
handkerchief. Smell, cousin.—He says he'll give me something that will make my smocks smell this way. Is not it

444 *daughter-in-law* step-daughter
444 *for* (to be Ww)
447 *liking of you* (liking you Ww)
452 *Are not you* (Are you not Q3, 4, Ww)
459 *peruke* an artificial cap of hair

pure? It's better than lavender, mun. I'm resolved I won't
let nurse put any more lavender among my smocks, ha,
cousin? 470

MRS. FRAIL

Fie, miss; amongst your linen, you must say. You must never
say smock.

MISS PRUE

Why, it is not bawdy, is it, cousin?

TATTLE

O, madam, you are too severe upon miss; you must not find
fault with her pretty simplicity, it becomes her strangely.— 475
Pretty miss, don't let 'em persuade you out of your
innocency.

MRS. FORESIGHT

O, damn you, toad! I wish you don't persuade her out of her
innocency.

TATTLE

Who, I, madam? O Lord, how can your ladyship have such a 480
thought? Sure, you don't know me?

MRS. FRAIL

Ah devil, sly devil.—He's as close, sister, as a confessor. He
thinks we don't observe him.

MRS. FORESIGHT

A cunning cur; how soon he could find out a fresh harmless
creature; and left us, sister, presently. 485

TATTLE

Upon reputation—

MRS. FORESIGHT

They're all so, sister, these men. They love to have the
spoiling of a young thing; they are as fond of it, as of being
first in the fashion, or of seeing a new play the first day. I
warrant it would break Mr. Tattle's heart to think that 490
anybody else should be beforehand with him.

TATTLE

O Lord, I swear I would not for the world—

MRS. FRAIL

O hang you; who'll believe you? You'd be hanged before
you'd confess. We know you.—She's very pretty! Lord,
what pure red and white! She looks so wholesome; ne'er 495
stir, I don't know, but I fancy, if I were a man—

MISS PRUE

How you love to jeer one, cousin.

MRS. FORESIGHT

Harkee, sister, by my soul, the girl is spoiled already. D'ye

think she'll ever endure a great lubberly tarpaulin? Gad, I
warrant you, she won't let him come near her after Mr.   500
Tattle.

MRS. FRAIL

O'my soul, I'm afraid not. Eh! filthy creature, that smells
all of pitch and tar!—Devil take you, you confounded toad,
why did you see her before she was married?

MRS. FORESIGHT

Nay, why did we let him? My husband will hang us. He'll   505
think we brought 'em acquainted.

MRS. FRAIL

Come, faith, let us be gone. If my brother Foresight should
find us with them, he'd think so, sure enough.

MRS. FORESIGHT

So he would. But then, leaving 'em together is as bad. And
he's such a sly devil, he'll never miss an opportunity.   510

MRS. FRAIL

I don't care; I won't be seen in't.

MRS. FORESIGHT

Well, if you should, Mr. Tattle, you'll have a world to
answer for. Remember I wash my hands of it; I'm
thoroughly innocent.

Exeunt MRS. FORESIGHT *and* MRS. FRAIL

[Act II, Scene xi]

MISS PRUE

What makes 'em go away, Mr. Tattle? What do they mean?   515
Do you know?

TATTLE

Yes, my dear, I think I can guess. But hang me if I know the
reason of it.

MISS PRUE

Come, must not we go too?

TATTLE

No, no, they don't mean that.   520

MISS PRUE

No! What then? What shall you and I do together?

TATTLE

I must make love to you, pretty miss; will you let me make
love to you?

MISS PRUE

Yes, if you please.

TATTLE (*Aside*)

    Frank, egad, at least. What a pox does Mrs. Foresight mean 525
by this civility? Is it to make a fool of me? Or does she leave
us together out of good morality, and do as she would be
done by? Gad, I'll understand it so.

MISS PRUE

    Well, and how will you make love to me? Come, I long to
have you begin. Must I make love too? You must tell me 530
how.

TATTLE

    You must let me speak miss, you must not speak first; I must
ask you questions, and you must answer.

MISS PRUE

    What, is it like the catechism? Come then, ask me.

TATTLE

    D'ye think you can love me? 535

MISS PRUE

    Yes.

TATTLE

    Pooh, pox, you must not say yes already; I shan't care a
farthing for you then in a twinkling.

MISS PRUE

    What must I say then?

TATTLE

    Why, you must say no, or you believe not, or you can't tell. 540

MISS PRUE

    Why, must I tell a lie then?

TATTLE

    Yes, if you would be well-bred. All well-bred persons lie.
Besides, you are a woman; you must never speak what you
think; your words must contradict your thoughts; but your
actions may contradict your words. So, when I ask you if you 545
can love me, you must say no, but you must love me too. If
I tell you you are handsome, you must deny it, and say I
flatter you. But you must think yourself more charming than
I speak you, and like me for the beauty which I say you have
as much as if I had it myself. If I ask you to kiss me, you 550
must be angry, but you must not refuse me. If I ask you for
more, you must be more angry, but more complying; and as
soon as ever I make you say you'll cry out, you must be sure
to hold your tongue.

542 *you would* (you'd Ww)

MISS PRUE

O Lord, I swear this is pure. I like it better than our old-   555
fashioned country way of speaking one's mind; and must
not you lie too?

TATTLE

Hum—yes—but you must believe I speak truth.

MISS PRUE

O Gemini! Well, I always had a great mind to tell lies, but
they frighted me, and said it was a sin.   560

TATTLE

Well, my pretty creature; will you make me happy by giving
me a kiss?

MISS PRUE

No, indeed; I'm angry at you.   *Runs and kisses him*

TATTLE

Hold, hold, that's pretty well, but you should not have given
it me, but have suffered me to take it.   565

MISS PRUE

Well, we'll do it again.

TATTLE

With all my heart. Now then, my little angel.   *Kisses her*

MISS PRUE

Pish.

TATTLE

That's right. Again, my charmer.   *Kisses again*

MISS PRUE

O fie, nay, now I can't abide you.   570

TATTLE

Admirable! That was as well as if you had been born and
bred in Covent Garden all the days of your life; and won't
you show me, pretty miss, where your bedchamber is?

MISS PRUE

No, indeed won't I: but I'll run there, and hide myself from
you behind the curtains.   575

TATTLE

I'll follow you.

MISS PRUE

Ah, but I'll hold the door with both hands, and be angry;
and you shall push me down before you come in.

TATTLE

No, I'll come in first, and push you down afterwards.

565 *to take* (to have taken Ww)
572 *all . . . life* (om. Ww)

MISS PRUE

   Will you? Then I'll be more angry, and more complying.   580

TATTLE

   Then I'll make you cry out.

MISS PRUE

   O, but you shan't, for I'll hold my tongue.

TATTLE

   O my dear, apt scholar.

MISS PRUE

   Well, now I'll run and make more haste than you.

                                        Exit MISS PRUE

TATTLE

   You shall not fly so fast, as I'll pursue.   *Exit after her*   585

[Act III, Scene i]

NURSE

   Miss, miss, Miss Prue. Mercy on me, marry and amen: why,
   what's become of the child? Why miss, Miss Foresight! Sure
   she has not locked herself up in her chamber and gone to
   sleep, or to prayers. Miss, miss! I hear her. Come to your
   father, child; open the door. Open the door, miss. I hear   5
   you cry husht. O Lord, who's there? (*Peeps*) What's here to
   do? O the Father! A man with her! Why, miss I say, God's
   my life, here's find doings towards—O Lord, we're all
   undone. O you young harlotry. (*Knocks*) Od's my life,
   won't you open the door? I'll come in the back way.   *Exit*   10

[Act III, Scene ii]

TATTLE *and* MISS PRUE *at the door*

MISS PRUE

   O Lord, she's coming, and she'll tell my father. What shall
   I do now?

TATTLE

   Pox take her; if she had stayed two minutes longer, I should
   have wished for her coming.

MISS PRUE

   O dear, what shall I say? Tell me, Mr. Tattle, tell me a lie.   15

TATTLE

   There's no occasion for a lie; I could never tell a lie to no

   3 *has not* (has Ww)
   10 s.d. *at the door* (om. Ww)

purpose. But since we have done nothing, we must say
nothing, I think. I hear her. I'll leave you together, and
come off as you can.   *Thrusts her in, and shuts the door*

[Act III, Scene iii]

Enter VALENTINE, SCANDAL, *and* ANGELICA

ANGELICA
You can't accuse me of inconstancy; I never told you that I   20
loved you.
VALENTINE
But I can accuse you of uncertainty, for not telling me
whether you did or no.
ANGELICA
You mistake indifference for uncertainty; I never had
concern enough to ask myself the question.   25
SCANDAL
Nor good nature enough to answer him that did ask you;
I'll say that for you, madam.
ANGELICA
What, are you setting up for good nature?
SCANDAL
Only for the affectation of it, as the women do for ill nature.
ANGELICA
Persuade your friend that it is all affectation.   30
VALENTINE
I shall receive no benefit from the opinion: for I know no
effectual difference between continued affectation and
reality.
TATTLE (*Coming up. Aside to* SCANDAL)
Scandal, are you in private discourse, anything of secrecy?
SCANDAL
Yes, but I dare trust you; we were talking of Angelica's love   35
for Valentine. You won't speak of it?
TATTLE
No, no, not a syllable. I know that's a secret, for it's
whispered everywhere.
SCANDAL
Ha, ha, ha.

23 *or no* (or not Ww)
31 s.p. VALENTINE (ANGELICA W1, SCANDAL W2)
36 *for Valentine* (to Valentine Ww)

ANGELICA

What is, Mr. Tattle? I heard you say something was   40
whispered everywhere.

SCANDAL

Your love of Valentine.

ANGELICA

How!

TATTLE

No, madam, his love for your ladyship. Gad take me, I beg
your pardon, for I never heard a word of your ladyship's   45
passion till this instant.

ANGELICA

My passion! And who told you of my passion, pray, sir?

SCANDAL

Why, is the devil in you? Did not I tell it you for a secret?

TATTLE

Gadso; but I thought she might have been trusted with her
own affairs.   50

SCANDAL

Is that your discretion? Trust a woman with herself?

TATTLE

You say true, I beg your pardon; I'll bring all off.—It was
impossible, madam, for me to imagine that a person of your
ladyship's wit and gallantry could have so long received the
passionate addresses of the accomplished Valentine, and yet   55
remain insensible; therefore, you will pardon me if from a
just weight of his merit, with your ladyship's good judgment,
I formed the balance of a reciprocal affection.

VALENTINE

O the devil, what damned costive poet has given thee this
lesson of fustian to get by rote?   60

ANGELICA

I dare swear you wrong him; it is his own. And Mr. Tattle
only judges of the success of others from the effects of his
own merit. For certainly Mr. Tattle was never denied
anything in his life.

TATTLE

O Lord! yes indeed, madam, several times.   65

ANGELICA

I swear I don't think 'tis possible

TATTLE

Yes, I vow and swear I have: Lord, madam, I'm the most

59 *costive* constipated; slow in his mental processes

unfortunate man in the world, and the most cruelly used by
the ladies.

ANGELICA

Nay, now you're ungrateful.   70

TATTLE

No, I hope not. 'Tis as much ingratitude to own some
favours, as to conceal others.

VALENTINE

There, now it's out.

ANGELICA

I don't understand you now. I thought you had never asked
anything, but what a lady might modestly grant, and you   75
confess.

SCANDAL

So, faith, your business is done here; now you may go brag
somewhere else.

TATTLE

Brag! O heavens! Why, did I name anybody?

ANGELICA

No; I suppose that is not in your power; but you would if   80
you could, no doubt on't.

TATTLE

Not in my power, madam! What, does your ladyship mean,
that I have no woman's reputation in my power?

SCANDAL (*Aside*)

Ouns, why you won't own it, will you?

TATTLE

Faith, madam, you're in the right; no more I have, as I hope 85
to be saved; I never had it in my power to say anything to a
lady's prejudice in my life. For as I was telling you, madam,
I have been the most unsuccessful creature living in things
of that nature, and never had the good fortune to be trusted
once with a lady's secret, not once.   90

ANGELICA

No?

VALENTINE

Not once, I dare answer for him.

SCANDAL

And I'll answer for him; for I'm sure if he had, he would
have told me. I find, madam, you don't know Mr. Tattle.

TATTLE

No indeed, madam, you don't know me at all I find: for sure   95
my intimate friends would have known—

ANGELICA

Then it seems you would have told, if you had been trusted.

TATTLE

O pox, Scandal, that was too far put.—Never have told
particulars, madam. Perhaps I might have talked as of a
third person, or have introduced an amour of my own in 100
conversation by way of novel; but never have explained
particulars.

ANGELICA

But whence comes the reputation of Mr. Tattle's secrecy, if
he was never trusted?

SCANDAL

Why thence it arises—the thing is proverbially spoken, but 105
may be applied to him—as if we should say in general terms,
he only is secret who never was trusted: a satirical proverb
upon our sex. There's another upon yours: as she is chaste
who was never asked the question. That's all.

VALENTINE

A couple of very civil proverbs, truly: 'tis hard to tell 110
whether the lady or Mr. Tattle be the more obliged to you.
For you found her virtue upon the backwardness of the men,
and his secrecy, upon the mistrust of the women.

TATTLE

Gad, it's very true, madam; I think we are obliged to acquit
ourselves. And for my part—but your ladyship is to speak 115
first—

ANGELICA

Am I? Well, I freely confess I have resisted a great deal of
temptation.

TATTLE

And I, gad, I have given some temptation that has not been
resisted. 120

VALENTINE

Good.

ANGELICA

I cite Valentine here, to declare to the court how fruitless
he has found his endeavours, and to confess all his solicitations and my denials.

VALENTINE

I am ready to plead, not guilty for you; and guilty for myself. 125

SCANDAL

So, why this is fair, here's demonstration with a witness.

TATTLE

Well, my witnesses are not present. But I confess I have had

favours from persons—but as the favours are numberless, so
the persons are nameless.

SCANDAL

Pooh, pox, this proves nothing.   130

TATTLE

No? I can show letters, lockets, pictures, and rings, and if
there be occasion for witnesses, I can summon the maids at
the chocolate-houses, all the porters of Pall Mall and
Covent Garden, the doorkeepers at the playhouse, the
drawers at Locket's, Pontack's, the Rummer, Spring-   135
Garden; my own landlady and *valet de chambre;* all who shall
make oath that I receive more letters than the secretary's
office; and that I have more vizor-masks to inquire for me
than ever went to see the hermaphrodite or the naked
prince. And it is notorious that in a country church, once, an   140
inquiry being made who I was, it was answered, I was the
famous Tattle, who had ruined so many women.

VALENTINE

It was there, I suppose, you got the nickname of the Great
Turk.

TATTLE

True; I was called Turk-Tattle all over the parish. The   145
next Sunday all the old women kept their daughters at
home, and the parson had not half his congregation. He
would have brought me into the spiritual court, but I was
revenged upon him, for he had a handsome daughter whom
I initiated into the science. But I repented it afterwards, for   150
it was talked of in town—and a lady of quality that shall be
nameless, in a raging fit of jealousy, came down in her coach
and six horses, and exposed herself upon my account; gad,
I was sorry for it with all my heart.—You know whom I
mean—you know where we raffled—   155

SCANDAL

Mum, Tattle,

VALENTINE

S'death, are not you ashamed?

130 *pox* (om. Ww)
133 *porters of* (porters at Ww)
135 *drawers* tapsters; barmen

139–40 *hermaphrodite . . . naked prince.* Popular shows of the day. The
'Prince' was the son of a 'King Moangis' (Summers).
155 *raffled.* I do not understand the allusion. Were they raffling for women
(or the reputation of having slept with them?).

ANGELICA

O barbarous! I never heard so insolent a piece of vanity. Fie,
Mr. Tattle, I'll swear I could not have believed it. Is this
your secrecy?   160

TATTLE

Gadso, the heat of my story carried me beyond my discretion, as the heat of the lady's passion hurried her beyond her
reputation. But I hope you don't know whom I mean, for
there were a great many ladies raffled.—Pox on't, now
could I bite off my tongue.   165

SCANDAL

No, don't; for then you'll tell us no more. (*Goes to the
door*) Come, I'll recommend a song to you upon the hint of
my two proverbs, and I see one in the next room that will
sing it.

TATTLE

For heaven's sake, if you do guess, say nothing. Gad, I'm   170
very unfortunate.

                    Re-enter SCANDAL, *with one to sing*

SCANDAL

Pray sing the first song in the last new play.

                              SONG
                    Set by Mr. John Eccles

A nymph and a swain to Apollo once prayed;
The swain had been jilted, the nymph been betrayed;
Their intent was to try if his oracle knew   175
E'er a nymph that was chaste, or a swain that was true.

Apollo was mute, and had like t'have been posed,
But sagely at length he this secret disclosed:
He alone won't betray in whom none will confide,
And the nymph may be chaste that has never been tried.   180

[Act III, Scene iv]

Enter SIR SAMPSON, MRS. FRAIL, MISS PRUE, *and* SERVANT

SIR SAMPSON

Is Ben come? Odso, my son Ben come? Odd, I'm glad on't.

166 *don't* Q3, 4, Ww (doubt on't Q1, 2)
177 *posed* puzzled

---

172 *Eccles.* (d.1735) He wrote the music for more than 40 plays, including
The Way of the World.

Where is he? I long to see him. Now, Mrs. Frail, you shall
see my son Ben. Body o'me, he's the hopes of my family. I
han't seen him these three years. I warrant he's grown.
Call him in; bid him make haste. I'm ready to cry for joy.   185

Exit SERVANT

MRS. FRAIL

Now, miss, you shall see your husband.

MISS PRUE (*Aside to* MRS. FRAIL)

Pish, he shall be none of my husband.

MRS. FRAIL

Hush. Well, he shan't, leave that to me.—I'll beckon Mr.
Tattle to us.

ANGELICA

Won't you stay and see your brother?   190

VALENTINE

We are the twin stars and cannot shine in one sphere: when
he rises I must set. Besides, if I should stay, I don't know
but my father in good nature may press one to the immediate
signing the deed of conveyance of my estate, and I'll defer it
so long as I can. Well, you'll come to a resolution.   195

ANGELICA

I can't. Resolution must come to me, or I shall never have
one.

SCANDAL

Come Valentine, I'll go with you; I've something in my
head to communicate to you.

Exit VALENTINE *and* SCANDAL

[Act III, Scene v]

SIR SAMPSON

What, is my son Valentine gone? What, is he sneaked off and   200
would not see his brother? There's an unnatural whelp!
There's an ill-natured dog! What, were you here too,
madam, and could not keep him! Could neither love, nor
duty, nor natural affection oblige him? Odsbud, madam,
have no more to say to him; he is not worth your considera-   205
tion. The rogue has not a dram of generous love about him:
all interest, all interest; he's an undone scoundrel, and

193 *one* Q1, 2 (me Q3, 4, Ww)

191 *twin stars*. Castor and Pollux. They were allowed by Zeus to dwell in
Heaven on alternate days.

courts your estate: body o'me, he does not care a doit for
your person.

ANGELICA

I'm pretty even with him, Sir Sampson, for if ever I could   210
have liked anything in him, it should have been his estate
too. But since that's gone, the bait's off, and the naked
hook appears.

SIR SAMPSON

Odsbud, well spoken, and you are a wiser woman than I
thought you were; for most young women nowadays are to   215
be tempted with a naked hook.

ANGELICA

If I marry, Sir Sampson, I'm for a good estate with any
man, and for any man with a good estate; therefore, if I
were obliged to make a choice, I declare I'd rather have you
than your son.   220

SIR SAMPSON

Faith and troth, you're a wise woman, and I'm glad to hear
you say so; I was afraid you were in love with the reprobate.
Odd, I was sorry for you with all my heart. Hang him, mon-
grel! Cast him off; you shall see the rogue show himself and
make love to some desponding Cadua of fourscore for   225
sustenance. Odd, I love to see a young spendthrift forced to
cling to an old woman for support, like ivy round a dead oak.
Faith, I do; I love to see 'em hug and cotton together, like
down upon a thistle.

[Act III, Scene vi]

Enter BEN LEGEND *and* SERVANT

BEN

Where's father?   230

SERVANT

There, sir, his back's toward you.

SIR SAMPSON

My son Ben! Bless thee, my dear boy; body o'me, thou art
heartily welcome.

BEN

Thank you, father, and I'm glad to see you.

208 *doit* a Dutch coin worth almost nothing
225 *Cadua* an obscure word, a windfall?
231 *toward* (towards W2)

SIR SAMPSON

Odsbud, and I'm glad to see thee. Kiss me, boy; kiss me;   235
again and again, dear Ben.   *Kisses him*

BEN

So, so, enough, father.—Mess, I'd rather kiss these gentle-
women.

SIR SAMPSON

And so thou shalt.—Mrs. Angelica, my son Ben.

BEN

Forsooth an you please. (*Salutes her*) Nay, mistress, I'm not   240
for dropping anchor here; about ship, i'faith. (*Kisses* MRS.
FRAIL) Nay, and you too, my little cockboat—so. (*Kisses*
MISS PRUE)

TATTLE

Sir, you're welcome ashore.

BEN

Thank you, thank you, friend.

SIR SAMPSON

Thou has been many a weary league, Ben, since I saw thee.   245

BEN

Ey, ey, been! Been far enough, an that be all.—Well, father,
and how do all at home? How does brother Dick, and brother
Val?

SIR SAMPSON

Dick, body o'me, Dick has been dead these two years; I writ
you word when you were at Leghorn.   250

BEN

Mess, and that's true; marry, I had forgot. Dick's dead, as
you say—well, and how? I have a many questions to ask
you. Well, you ben't married again, father, be you?

SIR SAMPSON

No, I intend you shall marry, Ben; I would not marry for
thy sake.   255

BEN

Nay, what does that signify? An you marry again—why then,
I'll go to sea again, so there's one for t'other, an that be all.
Pray don't let me be your hindrance; e'en marry, a God's
name, an the wind sit that way. As for my part, mayhap I
have no mind to marry.   260

MRS. FRAIL

That would be pity, such a handsome young gentleman.

240 *an you* (if you Ww)
251 *and that's* (that's Ww)

BEN

Handsome! he, he, he, nay, forsooth, an you be for joking,
I'll joke with you, for I love my jest, an the ship were sink-
ing, as we sayn at sea. But I'll tell you why I don't much
stand towards matrimony. I love to roam about from port   265
to port, and from land to land: I could never abide to be
port-bound, as we call it. Now a man that is married has, as
it were, d'ye see, his feet in the bilboes, and mayhap
mayn't get 'em out again when he would.

SIR SAMPSON

Ben's a wag.   270

BEN

A man that is married, d'ye see, is no more like another
man, than a galley slave is like one of us free sailors; he is
chained to an oar all his life, and mayhap forced to tug a
leaky vessel into the bargain.

SIR SAMPSON

A very wag, Ben's a very wag; only a little rough, he wants   275
a little polishing.

MRS. FRAIL

Not at all; I like his humour mightily, it's plain and honest.
I should like such a humour in a husband extremely.

BEN

Sayn you so, forsooth? Marry, and I should like such a
handsome gentlewoman for a bedfellow hugely. How say   280
you, mistress, would you like going to sea? Mess, you're a
tight vessel and well rigged, and you were but as well
manned.

MRS. FRAIL

I should not doubt that, if you were master of me.

BEN

But I'll tell you one thing, an you come to sea in a high   285
wind, or that lady [*To* ANGELICA], you mayn't carry so much
sail o'your head—top and top-gallant, by the mess.

MRS. FRAIL

No, why so?

BEN

Why an you do, you may run the risk to be overset, and then
you'll carry your keels above water, he, he, he.   290

---

268 *bilboes* fetters
287 *top and top-gallant* the sail set above the main mast and the sail
    above that

ANGELICA

I swear, Mr. Benjamin is the veriest wag in nature; an absolute sea-wit.

SIR SAMPSON

Nay, Ben has parts, but as I told you before, they want a little polishing: you must not take anything ill, madam.

BEN

No, I hope the gentlewoman is not angry; I mean all in good 295 part: for if I give a jest, I'll take a jest. And so forsooth you may be as free with me.

ANGELICA

I thank you, sir, I am not at all offended; but methinks, Sir Sampson, you should leave him alone with his mistress. Mr. Tattle, we must not hinder lovers.   300

TATTLE (*Aside to* MISS PRUE)

Well, miss, I have your promise.

SIR SAMPSON

Body o'me, madam, you say true. Look you Ben; this is your mistress. Come miss, you must not be shamefaced; we'll leave you together.

MISS PRUE

I can't abide to be left alone. Mayn't my cousin stay with 305 me?

SIR SAMPSON

No, no. Come, let's away.

BEN

Look you father, mayhap the young woman mayn't take a liking to me.

SIR SAMPSON

I warrant thee, boy. Come, come, we'll be gone; I'll 310 venture that.

Exeunt all but BEN *and* MISS PRUE

[Act III, Scene vii]

BEN

Come mistress, will you please to sit down, for an you stand astern a that'n, we shall never grapple together. Come, I'll haul a chair; there, an you please to sit, I'll sit by you.

MISS PRUE

You need not sit so near one; if you have anything to say, I 315 can hear you farther off, I an't deaf.

313 *astern a that'n* she has turned her back on him

BEN

Why, that's true, as you say, nor I an't dumb; I can be
heard as far as another. I'll heave off to please you. (*Sits
farther off*) An we were a league asunder, I'd undertake to
hold discourse with you, an 'twere not a main high wind   320
indeed, and full in my teeth. Look you forsooth, I am, as it
were, bound for the land of matrimony; 'tis a voyage, d'ye
see, that was none of my seeking. I was commanded by
father, and if you like of it, mayhap I may steer into your
harbour. How say you, mistress? The short of the thing is   325
this, that if you like me, and I like you, we may chance to
swing in a hammock together.

MISS PRUE

I don't know what to say to you, nor I don't care to speak
with you at all.

BEN

No, I'm sorry for that. But pray, why are you so scornful?   330

MISS PRUE

As long as one must not speak one's mind, one had better not
speak at all, I think, and truly I won't tell a lie for the
matter.

BEN

Nay, you say true in that; it's but a folly to lie: for to speak
one thing and to think just the contrary way is, as it were,   335
to look one way, and to row another. Now, for my part,
d'ye see, I'm for carrying things above board, I'm not for
keeping anything under hatches; so that if you ben't as
willing as I, say so, a God's name, there's no harm done;
mayhap you may be shamefaced; some maidens, tho'f they   340
love a man well enough, yet they don't care to tell'n so
to's face. If that's the case, why, silence gives consent.

MISS PRUE

But I'm sure it is not so, for I'll speak sooner than you
should believe that; and I'll speak truth, though one
should always tell a lie to a man; and I don't care, let my   345
father do what he will; I'm too big to be whipped, so I'll
tell you plainly, I don't like you, nor love you at all, nor
never will, that's more. So there's your answer for you, and
don't trouble me no more, you ugly thing.

BEN

Look you, young woman, you may learn to give good words,   350
however. I spoke you fair, d'ye see, and civil. As for your

325–6 *is this, that* (is, that Ww)

love or your liking, I don't value it of a rope's end; and
mayhap I like you as little as you do me: what I said was in
obedience to father; gad, I fear a whipping no more than you
do. But I tell you one thing, if you should give such language   355
at sea, you'd have a cat-o'-nine-tails laid cross your should-
ers. Flesh! who are you? You heard t'other handsome
young woman speak civilly to me of her own accord. Whatever you think of yourself, gad, I don't think you are any
more to compare to her, than a can of small beer to a bowl   360
of punch.

MISS PRUE

Well, and there's a handsome gentleman, and a fine gentleman, and a sweet gentleman, that was here that loves me, and
I love him; and if he sees you speak to me any more, he'll
thrash your jacket for you, he will, you great sea-calf.   365

BEN

What, do you mean that fair-weather spark that was here just
now? Will he thrash my jacket? Let'n—let'n. But an he
comes near me, mayhap I may giv'n a salt eel for's supper,
for all that. What does father mean to leave me alone as
soon as I come home with such a dirty dowdy? Sea-calf?   370
I an't calf enough to lick your chalked face, you cheese-curd
you. Marry thee! Ouns, I'll marry a Lapland witch as soon,
and live upon selling of contrary winds and wrecked vessels.

MISS PRUE

I won't be called names, nor I won't be abused thus, so I
won't. If I were a man, (*Cries*) you durst not talk at this   375
rate. No, you durst not, you stinking tar-barrel.

[Act III, Scene viii]

Enter MRS. FORESIGHT, *and* MRS. FRAIL

MRS. FORESIGHT

They have quarrelled just as we could wish.

BEN

Tar-barrel? Let your sweetheart there call me so, if he'll take
your part, your Tom Essence, and I'll say something to him;
gad, I'll lace his musk-doublet for him, I'll make him stink;   380

368 *salt eel* rope's end (a thrashing)
373 *selling of* (selling Ww)
379 *Tom Essence* a comedy by Thomas Rawlins (1676)

he shall smell more like a weasel than a civet cat afore I ha'
done with 'en.

MRS. FORESIGHT

Bless me, what's the matter? Miss—what, does she cry?—
Mr. Benjamin, what have you done to her?

BEN

Let her cry: the more she cries, the less she'll—She has been   385
gathering foul weather in her mouth, and now it rains out
at her eyes.

MRS. FORESIGHT

Come miss, come along with me, and tell me, poor child.

MRS. FRAIL

Lord, what shall we do? There's my brother Foresight and
Sir Sampson coming. Sister, do you take miss down into   390
the parlour, and I'll carry Mr. Benjamin into my chamber,
for they must not know that they are fallen out. Come sir,
will you venture yourself with me?   *Looks kindly on him*

BEN

Venture, mess, and that I will, though 'twere to sea in a
storm.   *Exeunt*   395

[Act III, Scene ix]

Enter SIR SAMPSON *and* FORESIGHT

SIR SAMPSON

I left 'em together here. What, are they gone? Ben's a brisk
boy: he has got her into a corner, father's own son! faith,
he'll tousle her, and mousle her: the rogue's sharp set,
coming from sea. If he should not stay for saying grace, old
Foresight, but fall to without the help of a parson, ha? Odd,   400
if he should, I could not be angry with him; 'twould be
but like me, a chip of the old block. Ha! thou'rt melancholy,
old prognostication; as melancholy as if thou hadst spilt the
salt or pared thy nails of a Sunday. Come cheer up, look
about thee. Look up, old stargazer. Now is he poring upon   405
the ground for a crooked pin, or an old horse-nail, with the
head towards him.

---

381 *civet cat* African and Asiatic animal from which the perfume
     civet was obtained
393 s.d. *Looks* (Looking Ww)
402 *melancholy* (melancholic Ww)
403 *melancholy* (melancholic Ww)
404 *of a* (on a Ww)

FORESIGHT
> Sir Sampson, we'll have the wedding tomorrow morning.

SIR SAMPSON
> With all my heart.

FORESIGHT
> At ten o'clock, punctually at ten.   410

SIR SAMPSON
> To a minute, to a second; thou shall set thy watch, and the
> bridegroom shall observe its motions; they shall be married
> to a minute, go to bed to a minute; and when the alarm
> strikes, they shall keep time like the figures of St. Dunstan's
> clock, and *consummatum est* shall ring all over the parish.   415

[Act III, Scene x]

Enter SCANDAL

SCANDAL
> Sir Sampson, sad news.

FORESIGHT
> Bless us!

SIR SAMPSON
> Why, what's the matter?

SCANDAL
> Can't you guess at what ought to afflict you and him, and all
> of us, more than anything else?   420

SIR SAMPSON
> Body o'me, I don't know any universal grievance, but a new
> tax and the loss of the Canary Fleet; without Popery should
> be landed in the west, or the French fleet were at anchor at
> Blackwall.

SCANDAL
> No. Undoubtedly Mr. Foresight knew all this, and might   425
> have prevented it.

FORESIGHT
> 'Tis no earthquake!

SCANDAL
> No, not yet; nor whirlwind. But we don't know what it may
> come to. But it has had a consequence already that touches
> us all.   430

---

415 *consummatum est* blasphemous i) it is finished ii) the marriage
    is consummated   422 *and* (or Ww)

422 *Canary Fleet* the French Fleet from the Canary Islands. England
    was at war with France   422 *without* (unless Ww)

SIR SAMPSON

Why, body o'me, out with't.

SCANDAL

Something has appeared to your son Valentine. He's gone to
bed upon't, and very ill. He speaks little, yet says he has a
world to say; asks for his father and the wise Foresight;
talks of Raymond Lully, and the ghost of Lilly. He has   435
secrets to impart, I suppose, to you two. I can get nothing
out of him but sighs. He desires he may see you in the
morning, but would not be disturbed tonight, because he has
some business to do in a dream.

SIR SAMPSON

Hoity toity! What have I to do with his dreams or his   440
divination? Body o'me, this is a trick to defer signing the
conveyance. I warrant the devil will tell him in a dream
that he must not part with his estate: but I'll bring him a
parson to tell him that the devil's a liar. Or if that won't
do, I'll bring a lawyer that shall out-lie the devil. And so I'll   445
try whether my blackguard or his shall get the better of the
day.   *Exit*

[Act III, Scene xi]

SCANDAL

Alas, Mr. Foresight, I'm afraid all is not right. You are a
wise man, and a conscientious man; a searcher into obscurity
and futurity; and if you commit an error, it is with a great   450
deal of consideration, and discretion, and caution.

FORESIGHT

Ah, good Mr. Scandal—

SCANDAL

Nay, nay, 'tis manifest; I do not flatter you. But Sir
Sampson is hasty, very hasty; I'm afraid he is not scrupulous
enough, Mr. Foresight. He has been wicked, and heaven   455
grant he may mean well in his affair with you—but my mind
misgives me, these things cannot be wholly insignificant.
You are wise, and should not be overreached, methinks you
should not—

433 *yet says* (yet he says Ww)

---

435 *Lully*. (?1235–1315) The philosopher, missionary, and linguist.
435 *Lilly*. (1602–81) Among the most famous of 17th-century English
    astrologers. He published an annual almanac, and was consulted by the
    Court. He predicted the Great Fire and Plague of London.

FORESIGHT

Alas, Mr. Scandal, *humanum est errare*. 460

SCANDAL

You say true, man will err; mere man will err—but you are something more. There have been wise men; but they were such as you: men who consulted the stars and were observers of omens. Solomon was wise, but how?—by his judgment in astrology. So says Pineda in his third book and eighth 465 chapter.

FORESIGHT

You are learned, Mr. Scandal!

SCANDAL

A trifler, but a lover of art—and the wise men of the east owed their instruction to a star, which is rightly observed by Gregory the Great in favour of astrology! And Albertus 470 Magnus makes it the most valuable science, because, says he, it teaches us to consider the causation of causes, in the causes of things.

FORESIGHT

I protest I honour you, Mr. Scandal. I did not think you had been read in these matters. Few young men are inclined— 475

SCANDAL

I thank my stars that have inclined me. But I fear this marriage and making over this estate, this transferring of a rightful inheritance, will bring judgments upon us. I prophesy it, and I would not have the fate of Cassandra, not to be believed. Valentine is disturbed; what can be the 480 cause of that? And Sir Sampson is hurried on by an unusual violence. I fear he does not act wholly from himself; methinks he does not look as he used to.

FORESIGHT

He was always of an impetuous nature. But as to this marriage, I have consulted the science, and all appearances 485 are prosperous.

468 *of art* (of the art Q4)
485 *science* (stars Q3, 4, Ww)

---

465 *Pineda.* (1557–1637) Spanish Jesuit and commentator on Solomon (Summers verifies the references).

470 *Gregory.* Pope 590–604, one of the four greater Doctors of the Western Church. Probably best known now for despatching St. Augustine to convert the English.

470–71 *Albertus Magnus.* (*c.*1200–80) Scholastic philosopher and polymath. He was the teacher of St. Thomas Aquinas.

SCANDAL

Come, come, Mr. Foresight, let not the prospect of worldly
lucre carry you beyond your judgment, nor against your
conscience. You are not satisfied that you act justly.

FORESIGHT

How!   490

SCANDAL

You are not satisfied, I say. I am loath to discourage you,
but it is palpable that you are not satisfied.

FORESIGHT

How does it appear, Mr. Scandal? I think I am very well
satisfied.

SCANDAL

Either you suffer yourself to deceive yourself, or you do   495
not know yourself.

FORESIGHT

Pray explain yourself.

SCANDAL

Do you sleep well o'nights?

FORESIGHT

Very well.

SCANDAL

Are you certain? You do not look so.   500

FORESIGHT

I am in health, I think.

SCANDAL

So was Valentine this morning, and looked just so.

FORESIGHT

How! Am I altered any way! I don't perceive it.

SCANDAL

That may be, but your beard is longer than it was two hours
ago.   505

FORESIGHT

Indeed! Bless me.

[Act III, Scene xii]

Enter MRS. FORESIGHT

MRS. FORESIGHT

Husband, will you go to bed? It's ten o'clock. Mr. Scandal,
your servant.

SCANDAL

Pox on her, she has interrupted my design. But I must work
her into the project.—You keep early hours, madam.   510

MRS. FORESIGHT

Mr. Foresight is punctual; we sit up after him.

FORESIGHT

My dear, pray lend me your glass, your little looking glass.

SCANDAL

Pray lend it him, madam. I'll tell you the reason. (*She gives
him the glass*; SCANDAL *and she whisper*) My passion for you is
grown so violent—that I am no longer master of myself. I   515
was interrupted in the morning, when you had charity
enough to give me your attention, and I had hopes of
finding another opportunity of explaining myself to you, but
was disappointed all this day; and the uneasiness that has
attended me ever since brings me now hither at this   520
unseasonable hour.

MRS. FORESIGHT

Was there ever such impudence, to make love to me before
my husband's face? I'll swear I'll tell him.

SCANDAL

Do, I'll die a martyr, rather than disclaim my passion. But
come a little farther this way, and I'll tell you what project I   525
had to get him out of the way, that I might have an
opportunity of waiting upon you.   *Whisper*

FORESIGHT (*Looking in the glass*)

I do not see any revolution here. Methinks I look with a
serene and benign aspect—pale, a little pale—but the roses
of these cheeks have been gathered many years. Ha! I do   530
not like that sudden flushing—gone already! Hem, hem,
hem! faintish. My heart is pretty good—yet it beats; and my
pulses, ha!—I have none—mercy on me! Hum—yes, here
they are. Gallop, gallop, gallop, gallop, gallop, gallop, hey!
Whither will they hurry me? Now they're gone again. And   535
now I'm faint again; and pale again, and hem! and my
hem!—breath, hem!—grows short; hem! hem! he, he, hem!

SCANDAL

It takes; pursue it in the name of love and pleasure.

MRS. FORESIGHT

How do you do, M₁. Foresight?

FORESIGHT

Hum, not so well as I thought I was. Lend me your hand.   540

SCANDAL

Look you there now. Your lady says your sleep has been
unquiet of late.

FORESIGHT

Very likely.

MRS. FORESIGHT
O, mighty restless, but I was afraid to tell him so. He has
been subject to talking and starting.   545
SCANDAL
And did not use to be so.
MRS. FORESIGHT
Never, never; till within these three nights; I cannot say
that he has once broken my rest since we have been married.
FORESIGHT
I will go to bed.
SCANDAL
Do so, Mr. Foresight, and say your prayers. He looks   550
better then he did.
MRS. FORESIGHT
Nurse, nurse!   *Calls*
FORESIGHT
Do you think so, Mr. Scandal?
SCANDAL
Yes, yes, I hope this will be gone by morning, taking it in
time.   555
FORESIGHT
I hope so.

[Act III, Scene xiii]

Enter NURSE

MRS. FORESIGHT
Nurse, your master is not well; put him to bed.
SCANDAL
I hope you will be able to see Valentine in the morning.
You had best take a little diacodium and cowslip water,
and lie upon your back; maybe you may dream.   560
FORESIGHT
I thank you, Mr. Scandal, I will.—Nurse, let me have a
watch-light, and lay the *Crumbs of Comfort* by me.
NURSE
Yes, sir.

554 *taking* (take W2)
559 *diacodium* syrup of poppies

562 *Crumbs of Comfort* (1628) by Michael Sparke. A popular work of
devotion. It ran through some forty or fifty editions in the first century
after its publication.

FORESIGHT

And—hem, hem! I am very faint.

SCANDAL

No, no, you look much better. 565

FORESIGHT

Do I? [*To* NURSE] And d'ye hear—bring me, let me see—
within a quarter of twelve—hem—he—hem!—just upon
the turning of the tide, bring me the urinal; and I hope
neither the lord of my ascendant nor the moon will be
combust; and then I may do well. 570

SCANDAL

I hope so. Leave that to me; I will erect a scheme; and I
hope I shall find both Sol and Venus in the sixth house.

FORESIGHT

I thank you, Mr. Scandal. Indeed, that would be a great
comfort to me. Hem, hem! Good night. *Exit*

[Act III, Scene xiv]

SCANDAL

Good night, good Mr. Foresight; and I hope Mars and 575
Venus will be in conjunction—while your wife and I are
together.

MRS. FORESIGHT

Well; and what use do you hope to make of this project?
You don't think that you are ever like to succeed in your
design upon me? 580

SCANDAL

Yes, faith I do; I have a better opinion both of you and
myself than to despair.

MRS. FORESIGHT

Did you ever hear such a toad? Harkee devil; do you think
any woman honest?

SCANDAL

Yes, several, very honest; they'll cheat a little at cards, 585
sometimes, but that's nothing.

MRS. FORESIGHT

Pshaw! but virtuous, I mean.

SCANDAL

Yes, faith, I believe some women are virtuous too; but 'tis

570 *combust* close to the sun, thus having their influence destroyed

---

572 *sixth house.* Virgo—perhaps another thrust at Foresight's impotence
(his wife is still a virgin).

as I believe some men are valiant, through fear. For why
should a man court danger, or a woman shun pleasure?   590

MRS. FORESIGHT

O monstrous! What are conscience and honour?

SCANDAL

Why, honour is a public enemy, and conscience a domestic
thief; and he that would secure his pleasure must pay a
tribute to one, and go halves with the t'other. As for
honour, that you have secured, for you have purchased a   595
perpetual opportunity for pleasure.

MRS. FORESIGHT

An opportunity for pleasure!

SCANDAL

Aye, your husband. A husband is an opportunity for
pleasure, so you have taken care of honour, and 'tis the
least I can do to take care of conscience.   600

MRS. FORESIGHT

And so you think we are free for one another?

SCANDAL

Yes, faith, I think so; I love to speak my mind.

MRS. FORESIGHT

Why then, I'll speak my mind. Now, as to this affair between
you and me. Here you make love to me; why, I'll confess
it does not displease me. Your person is well enough, and   605
your understanding is not amiss.

SCANDAL

I have no great opinion of myself; yet I think I'm neither
deformed, nor a fool.

MRS. FORESIGHT

But you have a villainous character; your are a libertine in
speech as well as practice.   610

SCANDAL

Come, I know what you would say. You think it more
dangerous to be seen in conversation with me, than to allow
some other men the last favour. You mistake; the liberty
I take in talking is purely affected for the service of your
sex. He that first cries out stop thief, is often he that has   615
stolen the treasure. I am a juggler that acts by confederacy;
and if you please, we'll put a trick upon the world.

MRS. FORESIGHT

Aye; but you are such a universal juggler—that I'm afraid
you have a great many confederates.

594 *with the t'other* (with t'other Q3, 4, Ww)
607 *yet I* (but I Ww)

SCANDAL

    Faith, I'm sound.   620

MRS. FORESIGHT

    O fie—I'll swear you're impudent.

SCANDAL

    I'll swear you're handsome.

MRS. FORESIGHT

    Pish, you'd tell me so, though you did not think so.

SCANDAL

    And you'd think so, though I should not tell you so: and now
I think we know one another pretty well.   625

MRS. FORESIGHT

    O Lord, who's here?

[Act III, Scene xv]

Enter MRS. FRAIL *and* BEN

BEN

    Mess, I love to speak my mind. Father has nothing to do
with me. Nay, I can't say that neither; he has something to
do with me. But what does that signify? If so be that I
ben't minded to be steered by him, 'tis as tho'f he should   630
strive against wind and tide.

MRS. FRAIL

    Aye, but, my dear, we must keep it secret, till the estate be
settled; for you know, marrying without an estate is like
sailing in a ship without ballast.

BEN

    He, he, he; why, that's true; just so, for all the world it is   635
indeed, as like as two cable ropes.

MRS. FRAIL

    And though I have a good portion, you know one would not
venture all in one bottom.

BEN

    Why, that's true again; for mayhap one bottom may spring a
leak. You have hit it indeed; mess, you've nicked the   640
channel.

MRS. FRAIL

    Well, but if you should forsake me after all, you'd break
my heart.

BEN

    Break your heart? I'd rather the *Marigold* should break her

620 *sound* free from venereal disease
621 *you're* (your Q1 uncorr. cited by Davis)

cable in a storm, as well as I love her. Flesh, you don't   645
think I'm false-hearted like a landman? A sailor will be
honest, tho'f mayhap he has never a penny of money in his
pocket. Mayhap I may not have so fair a face as a citizen or a
courtier; but for all that, I've as good blood in my veins, and
a heart as sound as a biscuit.   650

MRS. FRAIL
And will you love me always?

BEN
Nay, an I love once, I'll stick like pitch; I'll tell you that.
Come, I'll sing you a song of a sailor.

MRS. FRAIL
Hold, there's my sister; I'll call her to hear it.

MRS. FORESIGHT [*To* SCANDAL]
Well, I won't go to bed to my husband tonight, because I'll   655
retire to my own chamber and think of what you have said.

SCANDAL
Well, you'll give me leave to wait upon you to your chamber
door, and leave you my last instructions.

MRS. FORESIGHT
Hold, here's my sister coming toward us.

MRS. FRAIL
If it won't interrupt you, I'll entertain you with a song.   660

BEN
The song was made upon one of our ship's crew's wife; our
boatswain made the song; mayhap you may know her, sir.
Before she was married, she was called buxom Joan of
Deptford.

SCANDAL
I have heard of her.   665

                                              BEN *sings*

                     BALLAD
              Set by Mr. John Eccles
          A soldier and a sailor,
          A tinker, and a tailor,
          Had once a doubtful strife, sir,
          To make a maid a wife, sir,
          Whose name was buxom Joan.   670
          For now the time was ended,
          When she no more intended,
          To lick her lips at men, sir,

659 *toward* (towards Ww)
663 *was married* (married W2)

And gnaw the sheets in vain, sir,
And lie o'nights alone.   675

2.

The soldier swore like thunder,
He loved her more than plunder;
And showed her many a scar, sir,
That he had brought from far, sir,
With fighting for her sake.   680
The tailor thought to please her,
With off'ring her his measure.
The tinker too with mettle,
Said he could mend her kettle,
And stop up ev'ry leak.   685

3.

But while these three were prating,
The sailor slyly waiting,
Thought if it came about, sir,
That they should all fall out, sir:
He then might play his part.   690
And just e'en as he meant, sir,
To loggerheads they went, sir,
And then he let fly at her,
A shot 'twixt wind and water,
That won this fair maid's heart.   695

BEN

If some of our crew that came to see me are not gone, you
shall see that we sailors can dance sometimes as well as other
folks. (*Whistles*) I warrant that brings 'em, an they be
within hearing.

Enter SEAMEN

O, here they be—and fiddles along with 'em. Come my lads,   700
let's have a round, and I'll make one.   *Dance*
We're merry folk, we sailors; we han't much to care for. Thus
we live at sea: eat biscuit, and drink flip, put on a clean shirt
once a quarter, come home and lie with our landladies once
a year, get rid of a little money; and then put off with the   705
next fair wind. How d'ye like us?

MRS. FRAIL

O, you are the happiest, merriest men alive.

682 *measure* i) his yard ii) penis
703 *flip* a hot drink of sweetened beer and spirits

MRS. FORESIGHT

We're beholding to Mr. Benjamin for this entertainment.
I believe it's late.

BEN

Why, forsooth, an you think so, you had best go to bed. For   710
my part, I mean to toss a can, and remember my sweetheart,
afore I turn in; mayhap I may dream of her.

MRS. FORESIGHT

Mr. Scandal, you had best go to bed and dream too.

SCANDAL

Why, faith, I have a good lively imagination, and can dream
as much to the purpose as another, if I set about it: but   715
dreaming is the poor retreat of a lazy, hopeless, and imperfect lover; 'tis the last glimpse of love to worn-out sinners,
and the faint dawning of a bliss to wishing girls and growing
boys.

> There's nought but willing, waking love, that can   720
> Make blest the ripened maid, and finished man.

Exeunt

[Act IV, Scene i]

VALENTINE's *Lodging*

Enter SCANDAL *and* JEREMY

SCANDAL

Well, is your master ready? Does he look madly, and talk
madly?

JEREMY

Yes, sir; you need make no great doubt of that; he that was
so near turning poet yesterday morning can't be much to
seek in playing the madman today.   5

SCANDAL

Would he have Angelica acquainted with the reason of his
design?

JEREMY

No, sir, not yet. He has a mind to try whether his playing
the madman won't make her play the fool, and fall in love
with him; or at least own that she has loved him all this while   10
and concealed it.

SCANDAL

I saw her take coach just now with her maid, and think I
heard her bid the coachman drive hither.

708 *beholding* (beholden Ww)

JEREMY

Like enough, sir, for I told her maid this morning my master
was run stark mad only for love of her mistress. I hear a   15
coach stop; if it should be she, sir, I believe he would not
see her till he hears how she takes it.

SCANDAL

Well, I'll try her.—'Tis she, here she comes.

[Act IV, Scene ii]

Enter ANGELICA *with* JENNY

ANGELICA

Mr. Scandal, I suppose you don't think it a novelty to see a
woman visit a man at his own lodgings in a morning?   20

SCANDAL

Not upon a kind occasion, madam. But when a lady comes
tyrannically to insult a ruined lover, and make manifest
the cruel triumphs of her beauty, the barbarity of it
something surprises me.

ANGELICA

I don't like raillery from a serious face. Pray tell me what   25
is the matter?

JEREMY

No strange matter, madam; my master's mad, that's all. I
suppose your ladyship has thought him so a great while.

ANGELICA

How d'ye mean, mad?

JEREMY

Why, faith, madam, he's mad for want of his wits, just as   30
he was for want of money; his head is e'en as light as his
pockets, and anybody that has a mind to a bad bargain can't
do better than to beg him for his estate.

ANGELICA

If you speak truth, your endeavouring at wit is very
unseasonable—   35

SCANDAL (*Aside*)

She's concerned, and loves him.

ANGELICA

Mr. Scandal, you can't think me guilty of so much inhuman-
ity as not to be concerned for a man I must own myself
obliged to—pray tell me truth.

31 *was for* (was poor for Q3, 4, Ww)
39 *tell me truth* (tell me the truth W2)

SCANDAL

    Faith, madam, I wish telling a lie would mend the matter.   40
But this is no new effect of an unsuccessful passion.

ANGELICA (*Aside*)

    I know not what to think. Yet I should be vexed to have a
trick put upon me.—May I not see him?

SCANDAL

    I'm afraid the physician is not willing you should see him
yet.— Jeremy, go in and inquire.   *Exit* JEREMY   45

[Act IV, Scene iii]

ANGELICA (*Aside*)

    Ha! I saw him wink and smile. I fancy 'tis a trick! I'll
try.—I would disguise to all the world a failing, which I
must own to you. I fear my happiness depends upon the
recovery of Valentine. Therefore I conjure you, as you are
his friend, and as you have compassion upon one fearful of   50
affliction, to tell me what I am to hope for.—I cannot
speak.—But you may tell me; tell me, for you know what
I would ask.

SCANDAL (*Aside*)

    So, this is pretty plain.—Be not too much concerned,
madam; I hope his condition is not desperate: an acknow-   55
ledgment of love from you, perhaps, may work a cure, as the
fear of your aversion occasioned his distemper.

ANGELICA (*Aside*)

    Say you so; nay, then I'm convinced: and if I don't play
trick for trick, may I never taste the pleasure of revenge.—
Acknowledgment of love! I find you have mistaken my   60
compassion, and think me guilty of a weakness I am a
stranger to. But I have too much sincerity to deceive you, and
too much charity to suffer him to be deluded with vain
hopes. Good nature and humanity oblige me to be concerned
for him; but to love is neither in my power nor inclination;   65
and if he can't be cured without I suck the poison from his
wounds, I'm afraid he won't recover his senses till I lose
mine.

SCANDAL

    Hey, brave woman, i'faith—won't you see him then, if he
desire it?   70

52 *tell me; tell me, for* (tell me, for W2)

ANGELICA

What signify a madman's desires? Besides, 'twould make me
uneasy. If I don't see him, perhaps my concern for him may
lessen. If I forget him, 'tis no more than he has done by himself; and now the surprise is over, methinks I am not half so
sorry for him as I was.   75

SCANDAL

So, faith, good nature works apace; you were confessing
just now an obligation to his love.

ANGELICA

But I have considered that passions are unreasonable and
involuntary; if he loves, he can't help it; and if I don't love,
I can't help it; no more than he can help his being a man, or   80
I my being a woman; or no more than I can help my want of
inclination to stay longer here.—Come, Jenny.

Exit ANGELICA *and* JENNY

[Act IV, Scene iv]

SCANDAL

Humph! An admirable composition, faith, this same
womankind.

Enter JEREMY

JEREMY

What, is she gone, sir?   85

SCANDAL

Gone! Why, she was never here, nor anywhere else; nor I
don't know her if I see her, nor you neither.

JEREMY

Good lack! What's the matter now? Are any more of us to be
mad? Why, sir, my master longs to see her, and is almost
mad in good earnest with the joyful news of her being here.   90

SCANDAL

We are all under a mistake. Ask no questions, for I can't
resolve you; but I'll inform your master. In the meantime, if
our project succeed no better with his father than it does with
his mistress, he may descend from his exaltation of madness
into the road of common sense, and be content only to be   95
made a fool with other reasonable people. I hear Sir
Sampson. You know your cue; I'll to your master.   *Exit*

75 *sorry for him as* (sorry as Q3, 4, Ww)

[Act IV, Scene v]

Enter SIR SAMPSON LEGEND *with* [BUCKRAM] *a lawyer*

SIR SAMPSON

D'ye see, Mr. Buckram, here's the paper signed with his own
hand.

BUCKRAM

Good, sir. And the conveyance is ready drawn in this box, if   100
he be ready to sign and seal.

SIR SAMPSON

Ready, body o'me, he must be ready; his sham sickness
shan't excuse him.—O, here's his scoundrel. Sirrah, where's
your master?

JEREMY

Ah, sir, he's quite gone.   105

SIR SAMPSON

Gone! What, he is not dead?

JEREMY

No, sir, not dead.

SIR SAMPSON

What, is he gone out of town, run away, ha! Has he tricked
me? Speak, varlet.

JEREMY

No, no, sir; he's safe enough, sir, an he were but as sound,   110
poor gentleman. He is indeed here, sir, and not here, sir.

SIR SAMPSON

Hey day, rascal, do you banter me? Sirrah, d'ye banter me?
Speak, sirrah, where is he, for I will find him.

JEREMY

Would you could, sir, for he has lost himself. Indeed, sir,
I have almost broke my heart about him.—I can't refrain   115
tears when I think of him, sir; I'm as melancholy for him as
a passing-bell, sir, or a horse in a pound.

SIR SAMPSON

A pox confound your similitudes, sir. Speak to be understood, and tell me in plain terms what the matter is with
him, or I'll crack your fool's skull.   120

JEREMY

Ah, you've hit it, sir; that's the matter with him, sir; his
skull's cracked, poor gentleman; he's stark mad, sir.

SIR SAMPSON

Mad!

BUCKRAM

What, is he *non compos*?

JEREMY

Quite *non compos*, sir.   125

BUCKRAM

Why, then all's obliterated, Sir Sampson. If he be *non compos
mentis*, his act and deed will be of no effect; it is not good in
law.

SIR SAMPSON

Ouns, I won't believe it; let me see him, sir.—Mad! I'll
make him find his senses.   130

JEREMY

Mr. Scandal is with him, sir; I'll knock at the door.
Goes to the scene, which opens and discovers VALENTINE *upon
a couch disorderly dressed,* SCANDAL *by him*

[Act IV, Scene vi]

SIR SAMPSON

How now, what's here to do?

VALENTINE (*Starting*)

Ha! Who's that?

SCANDAL

For heaven's sake, softly, sir, and gently; don't provoke him.

VALENTINE

Answer me; who is that? and that?   135

SIR SAMPSON

Gads bobs, does he not know me? Is he mischievous? I'll
speak gently.—Val, Val, dost thou not know me, boy? Not
know thy own father, Val! I am thy own father, and this is
honest Brief Buckram the lawyer.

VALENTINE

It may be so—I did not know you.—The world is full.—   140
There are people that we do know, and people that we do not
know; and yet the sun shines upon all alike. There are
fathers that have many children, and there are children that
have many fathers.—'Tis strange! But I am Truth, and come
to give the world the lie.   145

SIR SAMPSON

Body o'me, I know not what to say to him.

VALENTINE

Why does that lawyer wear black? Does he carry his con-

138-9 *this is honest* (this honest W2)

science withoutside?—Lawyer, what are thou? Dost thou
know me?

BUCKRAM

O Lord, what must I say?—Yes, sir.   150

VALENTINE

Thou liest, for I am Truth. 'Tis hard I cannot get a liveli-
hood amongst you. I have been sworn out of Westminster
Hall the first day of every term. Let me see—no matter how
long. But I'll tell you one thing; it's a question that would
puzzle an arithmetician if you should ask him: whether the   155
Bible saves more souls in Westminster Abbey, or damns
more in Westminster Hall. For my part, I am Truth, and
can't tell; I have very few acquaintance.

SIR SAMPSON

Body o'me, he talks sensibly in his madness.—Has he no
intervals?   160

JEREMY

Very short, sir.

BUCKRAM

Sir, I can do you no service while he's in this condition;
here's your paper, sir. He may do me a mischief if I stay.
The conveyance is ready, sir, if he recover his senses. *Exit*

[Act IV, Scene vii]

SIR SAMPSON

Hold, hold, don't you go yet.   165

SCANDAL

You'd better let him go, sir, and send for him if there be
occasion, for I fancy his presence provokes him more.

VALENTINE

Is the lawyer gone? 'Tis well. Then we may drink about
without going together by the ears. Heigh ho! What o'clock
is't? My father here! Your blessing, sir?   170

SIR SAMPSON

He recovers.—Bless thee, Val. How dost thou do, boy?

VALENTINE

Thank you, sir, pretty well. I have been a little out of
order. Won't you please to sit, sir?

SIR SAMPSON

Aye, boy. Come, thou shalt sit down by me.

VALENTINE

Sir, 'tis my duty to wait.   175

152-3 *Westminster Hall* the principal law court

SIR SAMPSON

No, no, come, come, sit you down, honest Val. How dost
thou do? Let me feel thy pulse. O, pretty well now, Val.
Body' o'me, I was sorry to see thee indisposed; but I'm
glad thou'rt better, honest Val.

VALENTINE

I thank you, sir.   180

SCANDAL (*Aside*)

Miracle! The monster grows loving.

SIR SAMPSON

Let me feel thy hand again, Val. It does not shake. I believe
thou canst write, Val: ha, boy? Thou canst write thy name,
Val? (*In a whisper to* JEREMY) Jeremy, step and overtake Mr.
Buckram; bid him make haste back with the conveyance—   185
quick—quick.   *Exit* JEREMY

[Act IV, Scene viii]

SCANDAL (*Aside*)

That ever I should suspect such a heathen of any remorse!

SIR SAMPSON

Dost thou know this paper, Val? I know thou'rt honest and
wilt perform articles.

Shows him the paper, but holds it out of his reach

VALENTINE

Pray let me see it, sir. You hold it so far off that I can't tell   190
whether I know it or no.

SIR SAMPSON

See it, boy? Aye, aye, why thou dost see it. 'Tis thy own
hand, Val. Why, let me see, I can read it as plain as can be:
look you here, (*Reads*) *The condition of this obligation*—
Look you, as plain as can be, so it begins, and then at the   195
bottom, *As witness my hand*, VALENTINE LEGEND, in great
letters. Why, 'tis as plain as the nose in one's face; what, are
my eyes better than thine? I believe I can read it farther off
yet—let me see.

Stretches his arm as far as he can

VALENTINE

Will you please to let me hold it, sir?   200

SIR SAMPSON

Let thee hold it, sayst thou? Aye, with all my heart. What
matter is it who holds it? What need anybody hold it? I'll

176 *sit you* (sit thee Ww)
193 *Val* (Vally Ww)

put it up in my pocket, Val, and then nobody need hold it. (*Puts the paper in his pocket*) There Val: it's safe enough, boy. But thou shalt have it as soon as thou has set thy hand   205
to another paper, little Val.

[Act IV, Scene ix]

Re-enter JEREMY *with* BUCKRAM

VALENTINE

What, is my bad genius here again! O no, 'tis the lawyer with an itching palm, and he's come to be scratched. My nails are not long enough. Let me have a pair of red-hot tongs quickly, quickly, and you shall see me act St.   210
Dunstan, and lead the devil by the nose.

BUCKRAM

O Lord, let me be gone; I'll not venture myself with a madman.   *Exit* BUCKRAM

[Act IV, Scene x]

VALENTINE

Ha, ha, ha, you need not run so fast; honesty will not over-take you. Ha, ha, ha, the rogue found me out to be *in forma*   215
pauperis presently.

SIR SAMPSON

Ouns! What a vexation is here! I know not what to do, or say, nor which way to go.

VALENTINE

Who's that, that's out of his way?—I am Truth, and can set him right. Harkee, friend, the straight road is the worst   220
way you can go. He that follows his nose always will very often be led into a stink. *Probatum est.* But what are you for? Religion or politics? There's a couple of topics for you, no more like one another than oil and vinegar; and yet those two beaten together by a state-cook make sauce for the   225
whole nation.

SIR SAMPSON

What the devil had I to do ever to beget sons? Why did I ever marry?

VALENTINE

Because thou wert a monster, old boy: the two greatest

215–6 *in forma pauperis.* Perhaps a pun i) legally not liable for costs because
of poverty ii) in the image of a poor man.

monsters in the world are a man and a woman. What's thy   230
opinion?

SIR SAMPSON

Why, my opinion is, that those two monsters joined together
make yet a greater, that's a man and his wife.

VALENTINE

Aha! Old truepenny, sayst thou so? Thou hast nicked it.
But it's wonderful strange, Jeremy.   235

JEREMY

What is, sir?

VALENTINE

That grey hairs should cover a green head—and I make a
fool of my father.

   Enter FORESIGHT, MRS. FORESIGHT *and* MRS. FRAIL

What's here? *Erra pater*? Or a bearded sybil? If Prophecy
comes, Truth must give place.   *Exit with* JEREMY   240

[Act IV, Scene xi]

FORESIGHT

What says he? What, did he prophesy? Ha, Sir Sampson,
bless us! How are we?

SIR SAMPSON

Are we? A pox o' your prognostication. Why, we are fools
as we use to be. Ouns, that you could not foresee that the
moon would predominate, and my son be mad. Where's   245
your oppositions, your trines, and your quadrates? What did
your Cardan and your Ptolemy tell you? Your Messahalah
and your Longomontanus, your harmony of chiromancy
with astrology. Ah! pox on't, that I that know the world, and
men and manners, that don't believe a syllable in the sky   250
and stars, and sun and almanacs, and trash, should be
directed by a dreamer, an omen-hunter, and defer business
in expectation of a lucky hour, when, body o'me, there
never was a lucky hour after the first opportunity.

          Exit SIR SAMPSON

234 *truepenny* trusty fellow
239 *Erra pater* a fabulous astrologer
244 *use to be* (us'd to be W2)

247 *Cardan.* Jerome Cardan (1501–76) Italian mathematician, physician
  and astrologer.
248 *Longomontanus* (1562–1647), a Danish astronomer. Both he and Cardan
  combined an interest in mathematics with astrological calculation.

[Act IV, Scene xii]

FORESIGHT

Ah, Sir Sampson, heaven help your head. This is none of   255
your lucky hour; *nemo omnibus horis sapit*. What, is he gone,
and in contempt of science! Ill stars and unconverted
ignorance attend him.

SCANDAL

You must excuse his passion, Mr. Foresight, for he has been
heartily vexed. His son is *non compos mentis*, and thereby   260
incapable of making any conveyance in law; so that all his
measures are disappointed.

FORESIGHT

Ha! say you so?

MRS. FRAIL (*Aside to* MRS. FORESIGHT)

What, has my sea-lover lost his anchor of hope then?

MRS. FORESIGHT

O, sister, what will you do with him?   265

MRS. FRAIL

Do with him? Send him to sea again in the next foul weather.
He's used to an inconstant element, and won't be surprised
to see the tide turned.

FORESIGHT (*Considers*)

Wherein was I mistaken, not to foresee this?

SCANDAL (*Aside to* MRS. FORESIGHT)

Madam, you and I can tell him something else that he did   270
not foresee, and more particularly relating to his own
fortune.

MRS. FORESIGHT

What do you mean? I don't understand you.

SCANDAL

Hush, softly—the pleasures of last night, my dear, too
considerable to be forgot so soon.   275

MRS. FORESIGHT

Last night! And what would your impudence infer from last
night? Last night was like the night before, I think.

SCANDAL

S'death, do you make no difference between me and your
husband?

MRS. FORESIGHT

Not much. He's superstitious, and you are mad, in my   280
opinion.

256 *nemo . . . sapit* no one is wise all the time
257 *unconverted* (unconvertible Ww)

SCANDAL

You make me mad. You are not serious. Pray recollect
yourself.

MRS. FORESIGHT

O yes, now I remember. You were very impertinent and
impudent, and would have come to bed to me.   285

SCANDAL

And did not?

MRS. FORESIGHT

Did not! With that face can you ask the question?

SCANDAL [*Aside*]

This I have heard of before, but never believed. I have been
told she had that admirable quality of forgetting to a man's
face in the morning that she had lain with him all night,   290
and denying favours with more impudence than she could
grant 'em.—Madam, I'm your humble servant and honour
you.—You look pretty well, Mr. Foresight. How did you
rest last night?

FORESIGHT

Truly, Mr. Scandal, I was so taken up with broken dreams   295
and distracted visions that I remember little.

SCANDAL

'Twas a very forgetting night. But would you not talk with
Valentine? Perhaps you may understand him; I'm apt to
believe there is something mysterious in his discourses, and
sometimes rather think him inspired than mad.   300

FORESIGHT

You speak with singular good judgment, Mr. Scandal, truly.
I am inclining to your Turkish opinion in this matter, and do
reverence a man whom the vulgar think mad. Let us go in to
him.

MRS. FRAIL

Sister, do you stay with them; I'll find out my lover and   305
give him his discharge, and come to you. O'my conscience,
here he comes.

              Exeunt FORESIGHT, MRS. FORESIGHT, *and* SCANDAL

---

287 *that face* (what face W2)
291 *denying favours* (denying that she had done favours Ww)
303–4 *in to him* (to him Ww)

[Act IV, Scene xiii]

Enter BEN

BEN

All mad, I think. Flesh, I believe all the calentures of the sea
are come ashore, for my part.

MRS. FRAIL

Mr. Benjamin in choler!   310

BEN

No, I'm pleased well enough, now I have found you. Mess,
I've had such a hurricane upon your account yonder.

MRS FRAIL

My account! Pray, what's the matter?

BEN

Why, father came and found me squabbling with yon
chitty-faced thing, as he would have me marry; so he asked   315
what was the matter. He asked in a surly sort of a way. (It
seems brother Val is gone mad, and so that put'n into a
passion; but what did I know that, what's that to me?) So he
asked in a surly sort of manner, and gad I answered'n as surlily.
What tho'f he be my father, I an't bound prentice to 'en: so   320
faith, I told'n in plain terms, if I were minded to marry, I'd
marry to please myself, not him; and for the young woman
that he provided for me, I thought it more fitting for her to
learn her sampler, and make dirt-pies, than to look after a
husband; for my part I was none of her man. I had another   325
voyage to make, let him take it as he will.

MRS. FRAIL

So then you intend to go to sea again?

BEN

Nay, nay, my mind run upon you, but I would not tell him so
much. So he said he'd make my heart ache, and if so be that
he could get a woman to his mind, he'd marry himself. Gad,   330
says I, an you play the fool and marry at these years, there's
more danger of your head's aching than my heart. He was
woundy angry when I gav'n that wipe. He hadn't a word to
say, and so I left'n and the green girl together. Mayhap the
bee may bite and he'll marry her himself, with all my heart.   335

308 *calentures* fevers contracted by sailors in hot climates
315 *chitty-faced* baby-faced
324 *sampler* ornamental embroidery

MRS. FRAIL

And were you this undutiful and graceless wretch to your father?

BEN

Then why was he graceless first? If I am undutiful and graceless, why did he beget me so? I did not get myself.

MRS. FRAIL

O impiety! How have I been mistaken! What an inhuman 340 merciless creature have I set my heart upon? O, I am happy to have discovered the shelves and quicksands that lurk beneath that faithless smiling face.

BEN

Hey toss! What's the matter now? Why, you ben't angry, be you? 345

MRS. FRAIL

O, see me no more, for thou wert born amongst rocks, suckled by whales, cradled in a tempest, and whistled to by winds; and thou art come forth with fins and scales, and three rows of teeth, a most outrageous fish of prey.

BEN

O Lord, O Lord, she's mad, poor young woman! Love has 350 turned her senses, her brain is quite overset. Well-a-day, how shall I do to set her to rights?

MRS. FRAIL

No, no, I am not mad, monster; I am wise enough to find you out. Hadst thou the impudence to aspire at being a husband with that stubborn and disobedient temper? You that know 355 not how to submit to a father, presume to have a sufficient stock of duty to undergo a wife? I should have been finely fobbed indeed, very finely fobbed.

BEN

Harkee forsooth; if so be that you are in your right senses, d'ye see, for aught as I perceive I'm like to be finely fobbed 360 —if I have got anger here upon your account, and you are tacked about already. What d'ye mean, after all your fair speeches, and stroking my cheeks, and kissing and hugging, what, would you sheer off so? Would you, and leave me aground? 365

MRS. FRAIL

No, I'll leave you adrift, and go which way you will.

BEN

What, are you false-hearted then?

358 *fobbed* cheated

MRS. FRAIL

Only the wind's changed.

BEN

More shame for you—the wind's changed? It's an ill wind
blows nobody good. Mayhap I have good riddance on you,   370
if these be your tricks. What d'ye mean all this while, to make
a fool of me?

MRS. FRAIL

Any fool but a husband.

BEN

Husband! Gad, I would not be your husband, if you would
have me, now I know your mind, tho'f you had your weight   375
in gold and jewels and tho'f I loved you never so well.

MRS. FRAIL

Why, canst thou love, porpoise?

BEN

No matter what I can do. Don't call names—I don't love you
so well as to bear that, whatever I did. I'm glad you show
yourself, mistress. Let them marry you as don't know you.   380
Gad, I know you too well, by sad experience; I believe he
that marries you will go to sea in a hen-pecked frigate. I
believe that, young woman—and mayhap may come to an
anchor at Cuckold's Point; so there's a dash for you, take it
as you will. Mayhap you may holla after me when I won't   385
come to.   *Exit*

MRS. FRAIL

Ha, ha, ha, no doubt on't.—(*Sings*) *My true love is gone to
sea—*

[Act IV, Scene xiv]

Enter MRS. FORESIGHT

MRS. FRAIL

O, sister, had you come a minute sooner, you would have seen
the resolution of a lover. Honest Tar and I are parted; and   390
with the same indifference that we met. O'my life, I am half
vexed at the insensibility of a brute that I despised.

MRS. FORESIGHT

What then, he bore it most heroically?

370 *have good* (have a good Ww)
371 *d'ye* (did you Ww)
384 *Cuckold's Point* on the Thames at Rotherhithe

MRS. FRAIL

Most tyrannically, for you see he has got the start of me; and
I, the poor forsaken maid, am left complaining on the shore.   395
But I'll tell you a hint that he has given me: Sir Sampson is
enraged, and talks desperately of committing matrimony
himself. If he has a mind to throw himself away, he can't do
it more effectually than upon me, if we could bring it about.

MRS. FORESIGHT

O, hang him, old fox, he's too cunning; besides, he hates both   400
you and me. But I have a project in my head for you, and I
have gone a good way towards it. I have almost made a
bargain with Jeremy, Valentine's man, to sell his master to
us.

MRS. FRAIL

Sell him, how?   405

MRS. FORESIGHT

Valentine raves upon Angelica, and took me for her, and
Jeremy says will take anybody for her that he imposes on
him. Now I have promised him mountains, if in one of his
mad fits he will bring you to him in her stead, and get you
married together, and put to bed together; and after con-   410
summation, girl, there's no revoking. And if he should
recover his senses, he'll be glad at least to make you a good
settlement.—Here they come. Stand aside a little, and tell me
how you like the design.

[Act IV, Scene xv]

Enter VALENTINE, SCANDAL, FORESIGHT, *and* JEREMY

SCANDAL (*To* JEREMY)

And have you given your master a hint of their plot upon   415
him?

JEREMY

Yes, sir. He says he'll favour it, and mistake her for Angelica.

SCANDAL

It may make sport.

FORESIGHT

Mercy on us!

VALENTINE

Husht, interrupt me not—I'll whisper prediction to thee, and   420
thou shalt prophesy. I am Truth, and can teach thy tongue

418 *make sport* (make us sport Ww)

a new trick. I have told thee what's past, now I tell what's
to come. Dost thou know what will happen tomorrow?
Answer me not, for I will tell thee. Tomorrow knaves will
thrive through craft, and fools through fortune; and honesty　425
will go as it did, frost-nipped in a summer suit. Ask me
questions concerning tomorrow.

SCANDAL

Ask him, Mr. Foresight.

FORESIGHT

Pray, what will be done at court?

VALENTINE

Scandal will tell you; I am Truth, I never come there.　　430

FORESIGHT

In the city?

VALENTINE

O, prayers will be said in empty churches at the usual hours.
Yet you will see such zealous faces behind counters as if
religion were to be sold in every shop. O, things will go
methodically in the city; the clocks will strike twelve at　435
noon, and the horned herd buzz in the Exchange at two.
Wives and husbands will drive distinct trades, and care and
pleasure separately occupy the family. Coffee-houses will be
full of smoke and stratagem, and the cropt prentice, that
sweeps his master's shop in the morning, may ten to one,　440
dirty his sheets before night. But there are two things that
you will see very strange; which are wanton wives, with
their legs at liberty, and tame cuckolds, with chains about
their necks. But hold, I must examine you before I go
further; you look suspiciously. Are you a husband?　　445

FORESIGHT

I am married.

VALENTINE

Poor creature! Is your wife of Covent Garden parish?

FORESIGHT

No, St. Martin's-in-the-Fields.

VALENTINE

Alas, poor man; his eyes are sunk, and his hands shrivelled;
his legs dwindled, and his back bowed. Pray, pray, for a　450

---

422 *I tell* (I'll tell you Ww)
437 *Wives and husbands* (Husbands and wives W2)

---

447 *Covent Garden parish.* Covent Garden was notorious as a centre of
dissipation. Valentine suggests that Foresight's wife is a whore.

metamorphosis. Change thy shape, and shake off age; get
thee Medea's kettle, and be boiled anew; come forth with
labouring callous hands, a chine of steel, and Atlas' should-
ers. Let Taliacotius trim the calves of twenty chairmen,
and make thee pedestals to stand erect upon and look matri-   455
mony in the face. Ha, ha, ha! That a man should have a
stomach to a wedding supper, when the pigeons ought
rather to be laid to his feet, ha, ha, ha.

FORESIGHT
His frenzy is very high now, Mr. Scandal.

SCANDAL
I believe it is a spring tide.   460

FORESIGHT
Very likely truly; you understand these matters. Mr.
Scandal, I shall be very glad to confer with you about these
things which he has uttered. His sayings are very mysterious
and hieroglyphical.

VALENTINE
O, why would Angelica be absent from my eyes so long?   465

JEREMY
She's here, sir.

MRS. FORESIGHT
Now, sister.

MRS. FRAIL
O Lord, what must I say?

SCANDAL
Humour him, madam, by all means.

VALENTINE
Where is she? O, I see her. She comes, like riches, health,   470
and liberty at once, to a despairing, starving, and abandoned
wretch. O welcome, welcome.

MRS. FRAIL
How d'ye, sir? Can I serve you?

453 *chine* spine

---

452 *Medea's kettle.* The cauldron in which the Colchian witch Medea
prepared the magic herbs with which she restored youth to Jason's
father, Aeson.

454 *Taliacotius.* (1546–99) Bolognese surgeon famous for his experiments
in skin grafting.

457–8 *pigeons . . . feet.* A restorative for the dying, see Pepys' *Diary,* 19
October 1663, 'The Queen . . . . was so ill as to be shaved and pidgeons
put to her feet, and to have the extreme unction given her by the
priests'.

VALENTINE

Harkee, I have a secret to tell you—Endymion and the moon
shall meet us upon Mount Latmos, and we'll be married in   475
the dead of night—but say not a word. Hymen shall put his
torch into a dark lanthorn, that it may be secret; and Juno
shall give her peacock poppy-water, that he may fold his
ogling tail, and Argos's hundred eyes be shut, ha? Nobody
shall know but Jeremy.   480

MRS. FRAIL

No, no, we'll keep it secret; it shall be done presently.

VALENTINE

The sooner the better.—Jeremy, come hither—closer—
that none may overhear us. Jeremy, I can tell you news:
Angelica is turned nun, and I am turning friar, and yet we'll
marry one another in spite of the Pope. Get me a cowl and   485
beads that I may play my part, for she'll meet me two hours
hence in black and white, and a long veil to cover the project,
and we won't see one another's faces till we have done
something to be ashamed of; and then we'll blush once for
all.   490

[Act IV, Scene xvi]

Enter TATTLE *and* ANGELICA

JEREMY

I'll take care, and—

VALENTINE

Whisper.

ANGELICA

Nay, Mr. Tattle, if you make love to me, you spoil my
design, for I intended to make you my confidant.

TATTLE

But, madam, to throw away your person, such a person!   495
and such a fortune, on a madman!

ANGELICA

I never loved him till he was mad; but don't tell anybody so.

494 *intended* (intend Q3, 4, Ww)

---

474 *Endymion.* The shepherd with whom the moon fell in love as he slept
on Mount Latmos.
476–9 *Hymen . . . shut.* We shall be married in secret. Juno was protec-
toress of marriage. Argos was the hundred-eyed watchman she employed
to keep Jupiter from his mistress Io, but Mercury killed him. His eyes
were then placed in the peacock's tail.

SCANDAL

How's this! Tattle making love to Angelica!

TATTLE

Tell, madam! Alas, you don't know me. I have much ado to
tell your ladyship how long I have been in love with you,   500
but encouraged by the impossibility of Valentine's making
any more addresses to you, I have ventured to declare the
very inmost passion of my heart. O, madam, look upon us
both. There you see the ruins of a poor decayed creature,
here, a complete and lively figure, with youth and health,   505
and all his five senses in perfection, madam, and to all this,
the most passionate lover—

ANGELICA

O, fie for shame, hold your tongue; a passionate lover, and
five senses in perfection! When you are as mad as Valentine,
I'll believe you love me, and the maddest shall take me.   510

VALENTINE

It is enough. Ha! Who's here?

MRS. FRAIL (*To* JEREMY)

O Lord, her coming will spoil all.

JEREMY

No, no, madam, he won't know her. If he should, I can
persuade him.

VALENTINE

Scandal, who are all these? Foreigners? If they are, I'll tell 515
you what I think. (*Whispers*) Get away all the company but
Angelica, that I may discover my design to her.

SCANDAL

I will. I have discovered something of Tattle, that is of a
piece with Mrs. Frail. He courts Angelica, if we could contrive to couple 'em together. Harkee.   *Whispers* 520

MRS. FORESIGHT

He won't know you, cousin; he knows nobody.

FORESIGHT

But he knows more than anybody. O, niece, he knows things
past and to come, and all the profound secrets of time.

TATTLE

Look you, Mr. Foresight, it is not my way to make many
words of matters, and so I shan't say much, but in short,   525
d'ye see, I will hold you a hundred pound now that I
know more secrets than he.

505 *complete and lively* (complete, lively W2)
515 *are all these?* (are these? Q3, 4, Ww)

FORESIGHT

How! I cannot read that knowledge in your face, Mr. Tattle.
Pray, what do you know?

TATTLE

Why d'ye think I'll tell you, sir! Read it in my face? No, sir,   530
'tis written in my heart. And safer there, sir, than letters
writ in juice of lemon, for no fire can fetch it out. I am no
blab, sir.

VALENTINE (*To* SCANDAL)

Acquaint Jeremy with it; he may easily bring it about. They
are welcome, and I'll tell 'em so myself.—What, do you look   535
strange upon me? Then I must be plain. (*Coming up to them*)
I am Truth, and hate an old acquaintance with a new face.

SCANDAL *goes aside with* JEREMY

TATTLE

Do you know me, Valentine?

VALENTINE

You? Who are you? No, I hope not.

TATTLE

I am Jack Tattle, your friend.   540

VALENTINE

My friend, what to do? I am no married man, and thou canst
not lie with my wife; I am very poor, and thou canst not
borrow money of me; then what employment have I for a
friend?

TATTLE

Hah! A good open speaker, and not to be trusted with a   545
secret.

ANGELICA

Do you know me, Valentine?

VALENTINE

O, very well.

ANGELICA

Who am I?

VALENTINE

You're a woman, one to whom heaven gave beauty when it   550
grafted roses on a briar. You are the reflection of heaven in a
pond, and he that leaps at you is sunk. You are all white, a
sheet of lovely spotless paper, when you first are born; but
you are to be scrawled and blotted by every goose's quill. I
know you; for I loved a woman, and loved her so long that   555
I found out a strange thing: I found out what a woman was
good for.

TATTLE
  Aye, prithee, what's that?
VALENTINE
  Why, to keep a secret.
TATTLE
  O Lord!   560
VALENTINE
  O exceeding good to keep a secret: for though she should
  tell, yet she is not to be believed.
TATTLE
  Hah! good again, faith.
VALENTINE
  I would have music. Sing me the song that I like.

                         SONG
                   Set by Mr. Finger
      I tell thee, Charmion, could I time retrieve,   565
      And could again begin to love and live,
      To you I should my earliest off'ring give;
        I know my eyes would lead my heart to you,
        And I should all my vows and oaths renew,
        But to be plain, I never would be true.   570

      For by our weak and weary truth, I find,
      Love hates to centre in a point assigned,
      But runs with joy the circle of the mind.
        Then never let us chain what should be free,
        But for relief of either sex agree,   575
        Since women love to change, and so do we.

VALENTINE (*Walks musing*)
  No more, for I am melancholy.
JEREMY (*To* SCANDAL)
  I'll do't, sir.
SCANDAL
  Mr. Foresight, we had best leave him. He may grow out-
  rageous and do mischief.   580
FORESIGHT
  I will be directed by you.
JEREMY (*To* MRS. FRAIL)
  You'll meet, madam, I'll take care everything shall be ready.

---

564 *Finger*. Godfrey Finger (1685–1717), a Moravian composer. He wrote
  a score for Congreve's *The Mourning Bride*.

MRS. FRAIL

   Thou shalt do what thou wilt, have what thou wilt; in short,
   I will deny thee nothing.

TATTLE (*To* ANGELICA)

   Madam, shall I wait upon you?   585

ANGELICA

   No, I'll stay with him; Mr. Scandal will protect me. Aunt,
   Mr. Tattle desires you would give him leave to wait on you.

TATTLE [*Aside*]

   Pox on't, there's no coming off, now she has said that.—
   Madam, will you do me the honour?

MRS. FORESIGHT

   Mr. Tattle might have used less ceremony.   590

                    Exeunt FORESIGHT, MRS. FORESIGHT, TATTLE,
                    MRS. FRAIL

[Act IV, Scene xvii]

SCANDAL

   Jeremy, follow Tattle.   *Exit* JEREMY

ANGELICA

   Mr. Scandal, I only stay till my maid comes, and because I
   had a mind to be rid of Mr. Tattle.

SCANDAL

   Madam, I am very glad that I overheard a better reason,
   which you gave to Mr. Tattle; for his impertinence forced   595
   you to acknowledge a kindness for Valentine, which you
   denied to all his sufferings and my solicitations. So I'll
   leave him to make use of the discovery, and your ladyship
   to the free confession of your inclinations.

ANGELICA

   O heavens! You won't leave me alone with a madman?   600

SCANDAL

   No, madam; I only leave a madman to his remedy.

                                            Exit SCANDAL

[Act IV, Scene xviii]

VALENTINE

   Madam, you need not be very much afraid, for I fancy I
   begin to come to myself.

ANGELICA (*Aside*)

   Aye, but if I don't fit you, I'll be hanged.

583 *have what thou wilt* (om. Ww)   604 *fit* punish, trick
5—LFL

VALENTINE

You see what disguises love makes us put on. Gods have 605
been in counterfeited shapes for the same reason, and the
divine part of me, my mind, has worn this mask of madness,
and this motley livery, only as the slave of love, and menial
creature of your beauty.

ANGELICA

Mercy on me, how he talks! Poor Valentine! 610

VALENTINE

Nay, faith, now let us understand one another, hypocrisy
apart. The comedy draws toward an end, and let us think of
leaving acting and be ourselves; and since you have loved
me, you must own I have at length deserved you should
confess it. 615

ANGELICA (*Sighs*)

I would I had loved you, for heaven knows I pity you; and
could I have foreseen the sad effects, I would have striven;
but that's too late.

VALENTINE

What sad effects? What's too late? My seeming madness has
deceived my father, and procured me time to think of means 620
to reconcile me to him and preserve the right of my inheritance to his estate, which otherwise by articles I must this
morning have resigned: and this I had informed you of
today, but you were gone before I knew you had been here.

ANGELICA

How! I thought your love of me had caused this transport 625
in your soul, which, it seems, you only counterfeited for
mercenary ends and sordid interest.

VALENTINE

Nay, now you do me wrong; for if any interest was considered, it was yours, since I thought I wanted more than
love to make me worthy of you. 630

ANGELICA

Then you thought me mercenary.—But how am I deluded
by this interval of sense, to reason with a madman?

VALENTINE

O, 'tis barbarous to misunderstand me longer.

617 *sad effects* (bad effects Q3, 4, Ww)
626–7 *for mercenary* (for by, mercenary Q1, 2; for by mercenary
    Q3, 4, W1)

[Act IV, Scene xix]

Enter JEREMY

ANGELICA

O, here's a reasonable creature.—Sure he will not have the
impudence to persevere.—Come, Jeremy, acknowledge　635
your trick, and confess your master's madness counterfeit.

JEREMY

Counterfeit, madam! I'll maintain him to be as absolutely
and substantially mad as any freeholder in Bethlehem; nay,
he's as mad as any projector, fanatic, chemist, lover, or poet
in Europe.　　　　　　　　　　　　　　　　　640

VALENTINE

Sirrah, you lie; I am not mad.

ANGELICA

Ha, ha, ha, you see he denies it.

JEREMY

O Lord, madam, did you ever know any madman mad
enough to own it?

VALENTINE

Sot, can't you apprehend?　　　　　　　　　　645

ANGELICA

Why, he talked very sensibly just now.

JEREMY

Yes, madam, he has intervals: but you see he begins to look
wild again now.

VALENTINE

Why, you thick-skulled rascal, I tell you the farce is done,
and I will be mad no longer.　　　　　*Beats him*　650

ANGELICA

Ha, ha, ha, is he mad, or no, Jeremy?

JEREMY

Partly, I think, for he does not know his mind two hours.
I'm sure I left him just now in a humour to be mad, and I
think I have not found him very quiet at this present.
(*One knocks*) Who's there?　　　　　　　　　655

VALENTINE

Go see, you sot.—I'm very glad that I can move your mirth,
though not your compassion.　　　　　*Exit* JEREMY

638 *Bethlehem* St. Mary of Bethlehem the lunatic asylum (Bedlam)
652 *his mind* (his own mind Ww)
653 *a humour* (the humour Ww)
657 s.d. *Exit* JEREMY (om. Ww)

ANGELICA

I did not think you had apprehension enough to be excep-
tious: but madmen show themselves most by overpretending
to a sound understanding, as drunken men do by over-acting   660
sobriety. I was half inclining to believe you, till I accidentally
touched upon your tender part; but now you have restored
me to my former opinion and compassion.

Enter JEREMY

JEREMY

Sir, your father has sent to know if you are any better yet.
Will you please to be mad, sir, or how?   665

VALENTINE

Stupidity! You know the penalty of all I'm worth must pay
for the confession of my senses; I'm mad, and will be mad to
everybody but this lady.

JEREMY

So, just the very backside of Truth. But lying is a figure in
speech that interlards the greatest part of my conversation.   670
—Madam, your ladyship's woman.   *Goes to the door*

[Act IV, Scene xx]

Enter JENNY

ANGELICA

Well, have you been there? Come hither.

JENNY

Yes, madam. (*Aside to* ANGELICA) Sir Sampson will wait
upon you presently.

VALENTINE

You are not leaving me in this uncertainty?   675

ANGELICA

Would anything but a madman complain of uncertainty?
Uncertainty and expectation are the joys of life. Security is
an insipid thing, and the overtaking and possessing of a wish
discovers the folly of the chase. Never let us know one
another better; for the pleasure of a masquerade is done   680
when we come to show faces. But I'll tell you two things
before I leave you: I am not the fool you take me for; and
you are mad and don't know it.

Exeunt ANGELICA *and* JENNY

663 s.d. *Enter* JEREMY (om. Ww)
681 *show faces* (show our faces Ww)

[Act IV, Scene xxi]

VALENTINE
From a riddle you can expect nothing but a riddle. There's
my instruction, and the moral of my lesson.   685

Re-enter JEREMY

JEREMY
What, is the lady gone again, sir? I hope you understood one
another before she went?

VALENTINE
Understood! She is harder to be understood than a piece of
Egyptian antiquity, or an Irish manuscript; you may pore
till you spoil your eyes, and not improve your knowledge.   690

JEREMY
I have heard 'em say, sir, they read hard Hebrew books
backwards; maybe you begin to read at the wrong end.

VALENTINE
They say so of a witch's prayer, and dreams and Dutch
almanacs are to be understood by contraries. But there's
regularity and method in that; she is a medal without a   695
reverse or inscription, for indifference has both sides alike.
Yet while she does not seem to hate me, I will pursue her,
and know her if it be possible, in spite of the opinion of
my satirical friend, Scandal, who says

    That women are like tricks by sleight of hand,   700
    Which, to admire, we should not understand.

            Exeunt

[Act V, Scene i]

A room in FORESIGHT'S *house*
Enter ANGELICA *and* JENNY

ANGELICA
Where is Sir Sampson? Did you not tell me he would be
here before me?

JENNY
He's at the great glass in the dining room, madam, setting his
cravat and wig.

ANGELICA
How! I'm glad on't. If he has a mind I should like him, it's   5
a sign he likes me; and that's more than half my design.

1 s.d. *room* (Rome Q1, 2)

JENNY

I hear him, madam.

ANGELICA

Leave me, and, d'ye hear, if Valentine should come, or send,
I am not to be spoken with.   *Exit* JENNY

[Act V, Scene ii]

Enter SIR SAMPSON

SIR SAMPSON

I have not been honoured with the commands of a fair lady   10
a great while—odd, madam, you have revived me—not
since I was five and thirty.

ANGELICA

Why, you have no great reason to complain, Sir Sampson;
that is not long ago.

SIR SAMPSON

Zooks, but it is, madam, a very great while; to a man that   15
admires a fine woman as much as I do.

ANGELICA

You're an absolute courtier, Sir Sampson.

SIR SAMPSON

Not at all, madam; odsbud, you wrong me: I am not so old,
neither, to be a bare courtier, only a man of words. Odd, I
have warm blood about me yet; I can serve a lady any way.   20
Come, come, let me tell you, you women think a man old too
soon, faith and troth you do. Come, don't despise fifty; odd,
fifty, in a hale constitution, is no such contemptible age.

ANGELICA

Fifty a contemptible age! Not at all, a very fashionable age I
think. I assure you I know very considerable beaux that set a   25
good face upon fifty. Fifty! I have seen fifty in a side box, by
candle-light, out-blossom five and twenty.

SIR SAMPSON

O pox, outsides, outsides, a pize take 'em, mere outsides.
Hang your side-box beaux; no, I'm none of those, none of
your forced trees, that pretend to blossom in the fall, and   30
bud when they should bring forth fruit. I am of a long-lived
race, and inherit vigour; none of my family married till

20 *I can* (and can Q3, 4, Ww)
28 *O pox* (om. Ww)
32 *family* (ancestors Ww)

fifty, yet they begot sons and daughters till fourscore. I am
of your patriarchs, I, a branch of one of your antediluvian
families, fellows that the flood could not wash away. Well,   35
madam, what are your commands? Has any young rogue
affronted you, and shall I cut his throat? or—

ANGELICA

No, Sir Sampson, I have no quarrel upon my hands; I have
more occasion for your conduct than your courage at this
time. To tell you the truth, I'm weary of living single, and   40
want a husband.

SIR SAMPSON

Odsbud, and 'tis pity you should. (*Aside*) Odd, would she
would like me; then I should hamper my young rogues; odd,
would she would; faith and troth, she's devilish handsome.
—Madam, you deserve a good husband, and 'twere pity you   45
should be thrown away upon any of these young idle rogues
about the town. Odd, there's ne'er a young fellow worth
hanging—that is a very young fellow. Pize on 'em, they never
think beforehand of anything; and if they commit matrimony, 'tis as they commit murder, out of a frolic; and are   50
ready to hang themselves, or to be hanged by the law, the
next morning. Odso, have a care, madam.

ANGELICA

Therefore I ask your advice, Sir Sampson: I have fortune
enough to make any man easy that I can like; if there were
such a thing as a young, agreeable man, with a reasonable   55
stock of good nature and sense—for I would neither have an
absolute wit, nor a fool.

SIR SAMPSON

Odd, you are hard to please, madam; to find a young fellow
that is neither a wit in his own eye, nor a fool in the eye of
the world, is a very hard task. But, faith and troth, you speak   60
very discreetly, for I hate both a wit and a fool.

ANGELICA

She that marries a fool, Sir Sampson, commits the reputation of her honesty or understanding to the censure of the
world; and she that marries a very witty man submits both to
the severity and insolent conduct of her husband. I should   65
like a man of wit for a lover, because I would have such an

45 *'twere pity* ('twere a pity Q4)
48 *that is* (that's Q2)
62–4 *commits . . . to the censure of the world* (forfeits Ww)
64 *submits both* (is a slave Ww)

one in my power; but I would no more be his wife than his
enemy; for his malice is not a more terrible consequence of
his aversion, than his jealousy is of his love.

SIR SAMPSON

None of old Foresight's sibyls ever uttered such a truth.   70
Odsbud, you have won my heart; I hate a wit—I had a son
that was spoiled among 'em; a good, hopeful lad, till he
learned to be a wit—and might have risen in the state. But,
a pox on't, his wit run him out of his money, and now his
poverty has run him out of his wits.   75

ANGELICA

Sir Sampson, as your friend, I must tell you, you are very
much abused in that matter; he's no more mad than you are.

SIR SAMPSON

How, madam! Would I could prove it.

ANGELICA

I can tell you how that may be done.—But it is a thing that
would make me appear to be too much concerned in your   80
affairs.

SIR SAMPSON (*Aside*)

Odsbud, I believe she likes me.—Ah, madam, all my affairs
are scarce worthy to be laid at your feet; and I wish, madam,
they stood in a better posture, that I might make a more
becoming offer to a lady of your incomparable beauty and   85
merit. If I had Peru in one hand and Mexico in t'other, and
the Eastern Empire under my feet, it would make me only a
more glorious victim to be offered at the shrine of your
beauty.

ANGELICA

Bless me, Sir Sampson, what's the matter?   90

SIR SAMPSON

Odd, madam, I love you, and if you would take my advice in
a husband—

ANGELICA

Hold, hold, Sir Sampson. I asked your advice for a husband,
and you are giving me your consent. I was indeed thinking
to propose something like it in a jest, to satisfy you about   95
Valentine: for if a match were seemingly carried on between
you and me, it would oblige him to throw off his disguise of
madness in apprehension of losing me, for you know he has
long pretended a passion for me.

84 *stood* (were Ww)
95 *a jest* (jest Q3, 4, Ww)

SIR SAMPSON

Gadzooks, a most ingenious contrivance—if we were to go   100
through with it. But why must the match only be seemingly
carried on? Odd, let it be a real contract.

ANGELICA

O fie, Sir Sampson, what would the world say?

SIR SAMPSON

Say, they would say, you were a wise woman, and I a happy
man. Odd, madam, I'll love you as long as I live, and leave   105
you a good jointure when I die.

ANGELICA

Aye, but that is not in your power, Sir Sampson; for when
Valentine confesses himself in his senses, he must make over
his inheritance to his younger brother.

SIR SAMPSON

Odd, you're cunning, a wary baggage! Faith and troth, I like   110
you the better. But, I warrant you, I have a proviso in the
obligation in favour of myself. Body o'me, I have a trick to
turn the settlement upon the issue male of our two bodies
begotten. Odsbud, let us find children, and I'll find an
estate.   115

ANGELICA

Will you? Well, do you find the estate, and leave the t'other
to me—

SIR SAMPSON

O rogue! But I'll trust you. And will you consent? Is it a
match then?

ANGELICA

Let me consult my lawyer concerning this obligation; and if I   120
find what you propose practicable, I'll give you my answer.

SIR SAMPSON

With all my heart. Come in with me, and I'll lend you the
bond. You shall consult your lawyer, and I'll consult a
parson. Odzooks, I'm a young man; odzooks, I'm a young
man, and I'll make it appear—Odd, you're devilish hand-   125
some; faith and troth, you're very handsome, and I'm very
young, and very lusty. Odsbud, hussy, you know how to
choose, and so do I. Odd, I think we are very well met. Give
me your hand; odd, let me kiss it; 'tis as warm and as soft—
as what?—odd, as t'other hand—give me t'other hand, and   130
I'll mumble 'em, and kiss 'em till they melt in my mouth.

116 *the t'other* (the other W2)
131 *mumble* munch without biting (he has no teeth?)

ANGELICA

Hold, Sir Sampson, you're profuse of your vigour before
your time: you'll spend your estate before you come to it.

SIR SAMPSON

No, no, only give you a rent-roll of my possessions—ah
baggage!—I warrant you, for little Sampson. Odd, Samp-   135
son's a very good name for an able fellow: your Sampsons
were strong dogs from the beginning.

ANGELICA

Have a care, and don't over-act your part. If you remember,
the strongest Sampson of your name pulled an old house
over his head at last.   140

SIR SAMPSON

Say you so, hussy? Come, let's go then. Odd, I long to be
pulling down too, come away. Odso, here's somebody
coming.   *Exeunt*

[Act V, Scene iii]

Enter TATTLE *and* JEREMY

TATTLE

Is not that she, gone out just now?

JEREMY

Aye, sir, she's just going to the place of appointment. Ah,   145
sir, if you are not very faithful and close in this business,
you'll certainly be the death of a person that has a most
extraordinary passion for your honour's service.

TATTLE

Aye, who's that?

JEREMY

Even my unworthy self, sir. Sir, I have had an appetite to be 150
fed with your commands a great while; and now, sir, my
former master having much troubled the fountain of his
understanding, it is a very plausible occasion for me to
quench my thirst at the spring of your bounty. I thought I
could not recommend myself better to you, sir, than by the   155
delivery of a great beauty and fortune into your arms, whom
I have heard you sigh for.

TATTLE

I'll make thy fortune; say no more. Thou art a pretty fellow,
and canst carry a message to a lady in a pretty soft kind of
phrase, and with a good persuading accent.   160

139 *the strongest . . . name* (Sampson, the strongest of the name Ww)
142 *pulling down* (pulling Ww)

JEREMY

Sir, I have the seeds of rhetoric and oratory in my head—I have been at Cambridge.

TATTLE

Aye, 'tis well enough for a servant to be bred at an university, but the education is a little too pedantic for a gentleman. I hope you are secret in your nature, private, close, ha?   165

JEREMY

O, sir, for that, sir, 'tis my chief talent; I'm as secret as the head of Nilus.

TATTLE

Aye? Who's he, though? A Privy Counsellor?

JEREMY (*Aside*)

O ignorance!—A cunning Egyptian, sir, that with his arms would overrun the country, yet nobody could ever find out   170 his headquarters.

TATTLE

Close dog! A good whoremaster, I warrant him.—The time draws nigh, Jeremy. Angelica will be veiled like a nun, and I must be hooded like a friar, ha, Jeremy?

JEREMY

Aye, sir, hooded like a hawk, to seize at first sight upon the   175 quarry. It is the whim of my master's madness to be so dressed; and she is so in love with him, she'll comply with anything to please him. Poor lady, I'm sure she'll have reason to pray for me, when she finds what a happy exchange she has made between a madman and so accomplished a   180 gentleman.

TATTLE

Aye, faith, so she will, Jeremy: you're a good friend to her, poor creature. I swear I do it hardly so much in consideration of myself, as compassion to her.

JEREMY

'Tis an act of charity, sir, to save a fine woman with 30,000   185 pound from throwing herself away.

TATTLE

So 'tis, faith. I might have saved several others in my time; but, egad, I could never find in my heart to marry anybody before.

JEREMY

Well, sir, I'll go and tell her my master's coming; and meet   190

---

167 *head of Nilus.* The source of the Nile was not determined until the mid-19th century.

you in half a quarter of an hour, with your disguise, at your own lodgings. You must talk a little madly; she won't distinguish the tone of your voice.

TATTLE

No, no, let me alone for a counterfeit; I'll be ready for you.

[Act V, Scene iv]

Enter MISS PRUE

MISS PRUE

O, Mr. Tattle, are you here! I'm glad I have found you; I   195
have been looking up and down for you like anything, till
I'm as tired as anything in the world.

TATTLE (*Aside*)

O pox, how shall I get rid of this foolish girl?

MISS PRUE

O, I have pure news; I can tell you pure news. I must not
marry the seaman now; my father says so. Why won't you be   200
my husband? You say you love me, and you won't be my
husband. And I know you may be my husband now if you
please.

TATTLE

O fie, miss; who told you so, child?

MISS PRUE

Why, my father. I told him that you loved me.   205

TATTLE

O fie, miss, why did you do so? And who told you so, child?

MISS PRUE

Who? Why, you did; did not you?

TATTLE

O pox, that was yesterday, miss; that was a great while ago,
child. I have been asleep since; slept a whole night, and did
not so much as dream of the matter.   210

MISS PRUE

Pshaw. O, but I dreamt that it was so, though.

TATTLE

Aye, but your father will tell you that dreams come by contraries, child. O fie; what, we must not love one another now;
pshaw, that would be a foolish thing indeed. Fie, fie, you're a
woman now, and must think of a new man every morning,   215
and forget him every night. No, no, to marry is to be a child
again, and play with the same rattle always. O fie, marrying
is a paw thing.

218 *paw* obscene

MISS PRUE

    Well, but don't you love me as well as you did last night,
then?   220

TATTLE

    No, no, child, you would not have me.

MISS PRUE

    No? Yes, but I would, though.

TATTLE

    Pshaw, but I tell you, you would not. You forget you're a
woman and don't know your own mind.

MISS PRUE

    But here's my father, and he knows my mind.   225

[Act V, Scene v]

Enter FORESIGHT

FORESIGHT

    O, Mr. Tattle, your servant. You are a close man, but
methinks your love to my daughter was a secret I might have
been trusted with—or had you a mind to try if I could discover it by my art. Hum, ha! I think there is something in
your physiognomy that has a resemblance of her; and the   230
girl is like me.

TATTLE

    And so you would infer that you and I are alike.   (*Aside*)
What does the old prig mean? I'll banter him, and laugh at
him, and leave him.—I fancy you have a wrong notion of
faces.   235

FORESIGHT

    How? What? A wrong notion! How so?

TATTLE

    In the way of art. I have some taking features, not obvious
to vulgar eyes, that are indications of a sudden turn of good
fortune in the lottery of wives, and promise a great beauty
and great fortune reserved alone for me, by a private intrigue 240
of destiny, kept secret from the piercing eye of perspicuity,
from all astrologers and the stars themselves.

FORESIGHT

    How! I will make it appear that what you say is impossible.

TATTLE

    Sir, I beg your pardon; I'm in haste—

FORESIGHT

    For what?   245

239 *promise a* (promise of Q2–4)

TATTLE

To be married, sir, married.

FORESIGHT

Aye, but pray take me along with you, sir—

TATTLE

No, sir; 'tis to be done privately. I never make confidants.

FORESIGHT

Well; but my consent, I mean. You won't marry my daughter without my consent? 250

TATTLE

Who, I, sir? I'm an absolute stranger to you and your daughter, sir.

FORESIGHT

Hey day! What time of the moon is this?

TATTLE

Very true, sir, and desire to continue so. I have no more love for your daughter than I have likeness of you; and I have a 255 secret in my heart, which you would be glad to know, and shan't know; and yet you shall know it too, and be sorry for't afterwards. I'd have you to know, sir, that I am as knowing as the stars, and as secret as the night. And I'm going to be married just now, yet did not know of it half an hour ago; 260 and the lady stays for me, and does not know of it yet. There's a mystery for you.—I know you love to untie difficulties. Or if you can't solve this, stay here a quarter of an hour, and I'll come and explain it to you. *Exit*

[Act V, Scene vi]

MISS PRUE

O, father, why will you let him go? Won't you make him be 265 my husband?

FORESIGHT

Mercy on us, what do these lunacies portend? Alas! he's mad, child, stark wild.

MISS PRUE

What, and must not I have e'er a husband then? What, must I go to bed to nurse again, and be a child as long as she's an 270 old woman? Indeed, but I won't: for now my mind is set upon a man, I will have a man some way or other. O! methinks I'm sick when I think of a man; and if I can't have one, I would go to sleep all my life, for when I'm awake, it

265 *him be* (him to be Q3, 4, Ww)

makes me wish and long, and I don't know for what—and   275
I'd rather be always asleeping, than sick with thinking.

FORESIGHT

O fearful! I think the girl's influenced too.—Hussy, you
shall have a rod.

MISS PRUE

A fiddle of a rod, I'll have a husband; and if you won't get
me one, I'll get one for myself: I'll marry our Robin, the   280
butler. He says he loves me, and he's a handsome man, and
shall be my husband. I warrant he'll be my husband and
thank me too, for he told me so.

[Act V, Scene vii]

Enter SCANDAL, MRS. FORESIGHT, *and* NURSE

FORESIGHT

Did he so—I'll dispatch him for't presently. Rogue!— O,
nurse, come hither.   285

NURSE

What is your worship's pleasure?

FORESIGHT

Here, take your young mistress, and lock her up presently,
till further orders from me. Not a word, hussy; do what I
bid you; no reply, away. And bid Robin make ready to give
an account of his plate and linen; d'ye hear, be gone when   290
I bid you.

Exeunt NURSE *and* MISS PRUE

MRS. FORESIGHT

What's the matter, husband?

FORESIGHT

'Tis not convenient to tell you now.—Mr. Scandal, heaven
keep us all in our senses; I fear there is a contagious frenzy
abroad. How does Valentine?   295

SCANDAL

O, I hope he will do well again. I have a message from him to
your niece Angelica.

FORESIGHT

I think she has not returned since she went abroad with Sir
Sampson.

276 *always asleeping* (always asleep Q3, 4, Ww)
291 s.d. *Exeunt* NURSE *and* MISS PRUE (om. Ww, but add at the end of
     the scene; Nurse, why are you not gone?)

[Act V, Scene viii]

Enter BEN

MRS. FORESIGHT

Here's Mr. Benjamin, he can tell us if his father be come   300
home.

BEN

Who, father? Aye he's come home with a vengeance.

MRS. FORESIGHT

Why, what's the matter.

BEN

Matter! Why, he's mad.

FORESIGHT

Mercy on us, I was afraid of this.   305

BEN

And there's the handsome young woman, she, as they say,
brother Val went mad for; she's mad too, I think.

FORESIGHT

O my poor niece, my poor niece, is she gone too? Well, I
shall run mad next.

MRS. FORESIGHT

Well, but how mad? How d'ye mean?   310

BEN

Nay, I'll give you leave to guess. I'll undertake to make a
voyage to Antigua; no, hold, I mayn't say so neither—but
I'll sail as far as Leghorn and back again, before you shall
guess at the matter, and do nothing else; mess, you may take
in all the points of the compass, and not hit right.   315

MRS. FORESIGHT

Your experiment will take up a little too much time.

BEN

Why then, I'll tell you: there's a new wedding upon the
stocks, and they two are a-going to be married to rights.

SCANDAL

Who?

BEN

Why, father and—the young woman. I can't hit of her name.   320

SCANDAL

Angelica?

BEN

Aye, the same.

312 *no, hold, I* (no, I W2)

MRS. FORESIGHT
  Sir Sampson and Angelica, impossible!

BEN
  That may be, but I'm sure it is as I tell you.

SCANDAL
  S'death, it's a jest. I can't believe it.   325

BEN
  Look you, friend, it's nothing to me whether you believe it or
  no. What I say is true; d'ye see, they are married, or just
  going to be married, I know not which.

FORESIGHT
  Well, but they are not mad, that is, not lunatic?

BEN
  I don't know what you may call madness, but she's mad for a   330
  husband, and he's horn-mad, I think, or they'd ne'er make
  a match together.—Here they come.

[Act V, Scene ix]

Enter SIR SAMPSON, ANGELICA, *with* BUCKRAM

SIR SAMPSON
  Where is this old soothsayer, this uncle of mine elect? Aha,
  old Foresight, uncle Foresight, wish me joy, uncle Foresight,
  double joy, both as uncle and astrologer; here's a conjunction   335
  that was not foretold in all your Ephemeris. The brightest
  star in the blue firmament—is shot from above, in a jelly of
  love, and so forth; and I'm lord of the ascendant. Odd,
  you're an old fellow, Foresight, uncle I mean, a very old
  fellow, uncle Foresight; and yet you shall live to dance at my   340
  wedding; faith and troth, you shall. Odd, we'll have the
  music of the spheres for thee, old Lilly, that we will, and
  thou shalt lead up a dance in *via lactea*.

FORESIGHT
  I'm thunderstruck! You are not married to my niece?

SIR SAMPSON
  Not absolutely married, uncle, but very near it; within a kiss   345
  of the matter, as you see.   *Kisses* ANGELICA

---

343 *via lactea* the Milky Way

336–8 *brightest star . . . jelly of love.* The star is Venus, the jelly Dryden's,
  from *Tyrannic Love* IV. i: 'And drop from above/In a jelly of love!'
  The play had been revived at the Theatre Royal 1694.

ANGELICA

'Tis very true indeed, uncle; I hope you'll be my father, and give me.

SIR SAMPSON

That he shall, or I'll burn his globes. Body o'me, he shall be thy father, I'll make him thy father, and thou shalt make   350
me a father, and I'll make thee a mother, and we'll beget sons and daughters enough to put the weekly bills out of countenance.

SCANDAL

Death and hell! Where's Valentine?   *Exit* SCANDAL

[Act V, Scene x]

MRS. FORESIGHT

This is so surprising—   355

SIR SAMPSON

How! What does my aunt say? Surprising, aunt? Not at all, for a young couple to make a match in winter. Not at all— it's a plot to undermine cold weather, and destroy that usurper of a bed called a warming pan.

MRS. FORESIGHT

I'm glad to hear you have so much fire in you, Sir Sampson.   360

BEN

Mess, I fear his fire's little better than tinder; mayhap it will only serve to light up a match for somebody else. The young woman's a handsome young woman, I can't deny it; but, father, if I might be your pilot in this case, you should not marry her. It's just the same thing as if so be you should sail   365
so far as the Straits without provision.

SIR SAMPSON

Who gave you authority to speak, sirrah? To your element, fish; be mute, fish, and to sea; rule your helm, sirrah, don't direct me.

BEN

Well, well, take you care of your own helm, or you mayn't   370
keep your own vessel steady.

SIR SAMPSON

Why, you impudent tarpaulin! Sirrah, do you bring your forecastle jests upon your father? But I shall be even with you: I won't give you a groat. Mr. Buckram, is the convey-

366 *Straits* of Gibraltar
370 *own* (new Q3, 4, Ww)

ance so worded that nothing can possibly descend to this 375
scoundrel? I would not so much as have him have the prospect of an estate, though there were no way to come to it, but
by the Northeast Passage.

BUCKRAM

Sir, it is drawn according to your directions; there is not the
least cranny of the law unstopt. 380

BEN

Lawyer, I believe there's many a cranny and leak unstopt in
your conscience. If so be that one had a pump to your bosom,
I believe we should discover a foul hold. They say a witch
will sail in a sieve, but I believe the devil would not venture
aboard o'your conscience. And that's for you. 385

SIR SAMPSON

Hold your tongue, sirrah. How now, who's there?

[Act V, Scene xi]

Enter TATTLE *and* MRS. FRAIL

MRS. FRAIL

O, sister, the most unlucky accident!

MRS. FORESIGHT

What's the matter?

TATTLE

O, the two most unfortunate poor creatures in the world we
are. 390

FORESIGHT

Bless us! How so?

MRS. FRAIL

Ah, Mr. Tattle and I, poor Mr. Tattle and I are—I can't
speak it out.

TATTLE

Nor I—but poor Mrs. Frail and I are—

MRS. FRAIL

Married. 395

MRS. FORESIGHT

Married! How?

TATTLE

Suddenly—before we knew where we were—that villain
Jeremy, by the help of disguises, tricked us into one another.

378 *Northeast Passage* the impossible route north of Russia to the east
386 *there?* (here? Ww)
387 *sister* (sir Q4)
394 *but poor* (poor Ww)

FORESIGHT

Why, you told me just now you went hence in haste to be
married. 400

ANGELICA

But I believe Mr. Tattle meant the favour to me; I thank
him.

TATTLE

I did; as I hope to be saved, madam, my intentions were
good. But this is the most cruel thing, to marry one does
not know how, nor why, nor wherefore. The devil take me if 405
ever I was so much concerned at anything in my life.

ANGELICA

'Tis very unhappy, if you don't care for one another.

TATTLE

The least in the world—that is for my part; I speak for
myself. Gad, I never had the least thought of serious kindness; I never liked anybody less in my life. Poor woman! 410
Gad, I'm sorry for her too, for I have no reason to hate her
neither; but I believe I shall lead her a damned sort of life.

MRS. FORESIGHT (*Aside to* MRS. FRAIL)

He's better than no husband at all, though he's a coxcomb.

MRS. FRAIL (*To her*)

Aye, aye, it's well it's no worse.—Nay, for my part I always
despised Mr. Tattle of all things; nothing but his being my 415
husband could have made me like him less.

TATTLE

Look you there, I thought as much. Pox on't, I wish we could
keep it secret. Why, I don't believe any of this company
would speak of it.

MRS. FRAIL

But, my dear, that's impossible; the parson and that rogue 420
Jeremy will publish it.

TATTLE

Aye, my dear; so they will, as you say.

ANGELICA

O, you'll agree very well in a little time; custom will make it
easy to you.

TATTLE

Easy! Pox on't, I don't believe I shall sleep tonight. 425

SIR SAMPSON

Sleep, quotha! No! Why you would not sleep o'your wedding night? I'm an older fellow than you, and don't mean to
sleep.

BEN

Why, there's another match now, as tho'f a couple of
privateers were looking for a prize, and should fall foul of　430
one another. I'm sorry for the young man with all my heart.
Look you, friend, if I may advise you, when she's going—
for that you must expect, I have experience of her—when
she's going, let her go. For no matrimony is tough enough to
hold her, and if she can't drag her anchor along with her,　435
she'll break her cable, I can tell you that. Who's here? The
madman?

[Scene the Last]

Enter VALENTINE *dressed*, SCANDAL, *and* JEREMY

VALENTINE

No, here's the fool; and if occasion be, I'll give it under my
hand.

SIR SAMPSON

How now?　　　　　　　　　　　　　　　　　　　　440

VALENTINE

Sir, I'm come to acknowledge my errors, and ask your
pardon.

SIR SAMPSON

What, have you found your senses at last then? In good
time, sir.

VALENTINE

You were abused, sir; I never was distracted.　　　　445

FORESIGHT

How! Not mad! Mr. Scandal?

SCANDAL

No really, sir; I'm his witness; it was all counterfeit.

VALENTINE

I thought I had reasons. But it was a poor contrivance; the
effect has shown it such.

SIR SAMPSON

Contrivance, what, to cheat me? To cheat your father!　450
Sirrah, could you hope to prosper?

VALENTINE

Indeed, I thought, sir, when the father endeavoured to undo
the son, it was a reasonable return of nature.

SIR SAMPSON

Very good, sir.—Mr. Buckram, are you ready?—Come, sir,
will you sign and seal?　　　　　　　　　　　　　　455

VALENTINE

If you please, sir; but first I would ask this lady one question.

SIR SAMPSON

Sir, you must ask my leave first. That lady, no, sir; you shall ask that lady no questions, till you have asked her blessing, sir; that lady is to be my wife.

VALENTINE

I have heard as much, sir; but I would have it from her own 460 mouth.

SIR SAMPSON

That's as much as to say I lie, sir, and you don't believe what I say.

VALENTINE

Pardon me, sir. But I reflect that I very lately counterfeited madness; I don't know but the frolic may go round.   465

SIR SAMPSON

Come, chuck, satisfy him, answer him.—Come, come, Mr. Buckram, the pen and ink.

BUCKRAM

Here it is, sir, with the deed; all is ready.

VALENTINE *goes to* ANGELICA

ANGELICA

'Tis true, you have a great while pretended love to me; nay, what if you were sincere? Still you must pardon me, if I 470 think my own inclinations have a better right to dispose of my person, than yours.

SIR SAMPSON

Are you answered now, sir?

VALENTINE

Yes, sir.

SIR SAMPSON

Where's your plot, sir, and your contrivance now, sir? Will 475 you sign, sir? Come, will you sign and seal?

VALENTINE

With all my heart, sir.

SCANDAL

S'death, you are not mad, indeed, to ruin yourself?

VALENTINE

I have been disappointed of my only hope; and he that loses hope may part with anything. I never valued fortune, but as it 480

457 *my leave* (me leave Q3, 4, Ww)
466 *Come, come, Mr.* (Come, Mr. W2)

was subservient to my pleasure; and my only pleasure was to
please this lady. I have made many vain attempts, and find
at last that nothing but my ruin can effect it: which, for that
reason, I will sign to—give me the paper.

ANGELICA (*Aside*)
Generous Valentine!   485

BUCKRAM
Here is the deed, sir.

VALENTINE
But where is the bond by which I am obliged to sign this?

BUCKRAM
Sir Sampson, you have it.

ANGELICA
No, I have it; and I'll use it as I would everything that is an
enemy to Valentine.   *Tears the paper*   490

SIR SAMPSON
How now!

VALENTINE
Ha!

ANGELICA (*To* VALENTINE)
Had I the world to give you, it could not make me worthy of
so generous and faithful a passion: here's my hand, my heart
was always yours, and struggled very hard to make this   495
utmost trial of your virtue.

VALENTINE
Between pleasure and amazement, I am lost—but on my
knees I take the blessing.

SIR SAMPSON
Ouns, what is the meaning of this?

BEN
Mess, here's the wind changed again. Father, you and I may   500
make a voyage together now.

ANGELICA
Well, Sir Sampson, since I have played you a trick, I'll advise
you how you may avoid such another. Learn to be a good
father, or you'll never get a second wife. I always loved your
son, and hated your unforgiving nature. I was resolved to   505
try him to the utmost; I have tried you too, and know you
both. You have not more faults than he has virtues; and 'tis
hardly more pleasure to me that I can make him and myself
happy, than that I can punish you.

VALENTINE
If my happiness could receive addition, this kind surprise   510
would make it double.

SIR SAMPSON

Ouns, you're a crocodile.

FORESIGHT

Really, Sir Sampson, this is a sudden eclipse—

SIR SAMPSON

You're an illiterate fool, and I'm another, and the stars are
liars; and if I had breath enough, I'd curse them and you,   515
myself, and everybody. Ouns, cullied, bubbled, jilted,
woman-bobbed at last.—I have not patience.

Exit SIR SAMPSON

TATTLE

If the gentleman is in this disorder for want of a wife, I can
spare him mine. (*To* JEREMY) O, are you there, sir? I'm
indebted to you for my happiness.   520

JEREMY

Sir, I ask you ten thousand pardons, 'twas an arrant mistake.
You see, sir, my master was never mad, nor anything like it.
Then how could it be otherwise?

VALENTINE

Tattle, I thank you, you would have interposed between
me and heaven; but Providence laid purgatory in your way.   525
You have but justice.

SCANDAL

I hear the fiddles that Sir Sampson provided for his own
wedding; methinks 'tis pity they should not be employed
when the match is so much mended. Valentine, though it be
morning, we may have a dance.   530

VALENTINE

Anything, my friend, everything that looks like joy and
transport.

SCANDAL

Call 'em, Jeremy.

ANGELICA

I have done dissembling now, Valentine; and if that coldness
which I have always worn before you should turn to an   535
extreme fondness, you must not suspect it.

VALENTINE

I'll prevent that suspicion, for I intend to dote on at that

514 *illiterate fool* (illiterate old fool Ww)
514–17 *and the stars . . . patience* (om. Ww)
516 *cullied . . . jilted* deceived
517 s.d. *Exit* SIR SAMPSON (om. Ww)
518 *this disorder* (disorder Ww)
537–8 *on . . . rate* (to that immoderate degree Ww)

immoderate rate that your fondness shall never distinguish
itself enough to be taken notice of. If ever you seem to love
too much, it must be only when I can't love enough.　　540

ANGELICA

Have a care of large promises; you know you are apt to run
more in debt than you are able to pay.

VALENTINE

Therefore I yield my body as your prisoner, and make your
best on't.

SCANDAL

The music stays for you.　　545

Dance

Well, madam, you have done exemplary justice in punishing
an inhuman father, and rewarding a faithful lover; but there
is a third good work which I, in particular, must thank you
for: I was an infidel to your sex, and you have converted me.
For now I am convinced that all women are not like fortune,　　550
blind in bestowing favours, either on those who do not
merit, or who do not want 'em.

ANGELICA

'Tis an unreasonable accusation that you lay upon our sex:
you tax us with injustice, only to cover your own want of
merit. You would all have the reward of love, but few have　　555
the constancy to stay till it becomes your due. Men are
generally hypocrites and infidels; they pretend to worship,
but have neither zeal nor faith. How few, like Valentine,
would persevere even unto martyrdom, and sacrifice their
interest to their constancy! In admiring me, you misplace　　560
the novelty.
　　　　The miracle today is that we find
　　　　A lover true: not that a woman's kind.

　　　　　　　　　　　　　　　　　Exeunt Omnes

541 *large promises* (promises Q3, 4, Ww)
542 *able to pay* (able pay Q1)
559 *unto* (to Ww)

EPILOGUE

Spoken at the opening of the New House,
by Mrs. Bracegirdle

Sure Providence at first designed this place
To be the player's refuge in distress;
For still in every storm they all run hither,
As to a shed that shields 'em from the weather.
But thinking of this change which last befell us,   5
It's like what I have heard our poets tell us:
For when behind our scenes their suits are pleading,
To help their love, sometimes they show their reading;
And wanting ready cash to pay for hearts,
They top their learning on us, and their parts.   10
Once of philosophers they told us stories,
Whom, as I think they called—Py—Pythagories,
I'm sure 'tis some such Latin name they give 'em,
And we, who know no better, must believe 'em.
Now to these men (say they) such souls were given,   15
That after death ne'er went to hell, nor heaven,
But lived, I know not how, in beasts; and then,
When many years were past, in men again.
Methinks we players resemble such a soul,
That does from bodies, we from houses stroll.   20
Thus Aristotle's soul, of old that was,
May now be damned to animate an ass;
Or in this very house, for aught we know,
Is doing painful penance in some beau;
And this our audience, which did once resort   25
To shining theatres to see our sport,
Now find us tossed into a tennis court.
These walls but t'other day were filled with noise
Of roaring gamesters, and your Damme Boys.
Then bounding balls and racquets they encompassed,   30
And now they're filled with jests, and flights, and bombast!
I vow I don't much like this transmigration,
Strolling from place to place, by circulation.

25 *this* (thus Ww)

---

27 *tennis court.* The new Lincoln's Inn Theatre was in a converted tennis
court.

Grant heaven, we don't return to our first station.
I know not what these think, but for my part, 35
I can't reflect without an aching heart,
How we should end in our original, a cart.
But we can't fear, since you're so good to save us,
That you have only set us up, to leave us.
Thus from the past, we hope for future grace; 40
I beg it—
And some here know I have a begging face.
Then pray continue this your kind behaviour,
For a clear stage won't do, without your favour.

44 *clear stage* free from debt

---

37 *cart.* i) The cart on which plays were first performed, and possibly
ii) the cart which conveyed criminals to be hanged.

Printed in Great Britain by
The Garden City Press Limited
Letchworth, Hertfordshire